EDGAR CAYCE'S
PHOTOGRAPHIC LEGACY

Although today, even as in his time, few of his admirers realize it, Edgar Cayce was a professional photographer—and a good one, as this self-portrait shows—as well as a world-famous psychic, for which most people sought his services. This book offers memorabilia and many photographs by Edgar Cayce and others which present the Cayce life chronologically. Edgar was intrigued by self-portraiture. This one, for instance, was a photo postcard he sent to his wife, Gertrude, while his work separated them—she and baby Hugh Lynn in Anniston, Alabama, and he, with a bad cold, thirty miles away in Jacksonville, Alabama, working at the Russell Brothers studio. (Telephones were still a novelty and mail delivery took three or four days even for this distance.) The handwritten sign on the wall behind Edgar's chair reads: "Now is the time, this is the place. You are the girl to have your photo made today."

EDGAR CAYCE'S
PHOTOGRAPHIC LEGACY

Compiled, Correlated, and Captioned by

DAVID M. LEARY

DOUBLEDAY & COMPANY, INC., GARDEN CITY, NEW YORK 1978

Photographs and newsclippings courtesy of
the Edgar Cayce Foundation, except as noted below.
The psychic readings of Edgar Cayce are protected by copyright:
© 1971 Edgar Cayce Foundation. All rights reserved. The readings
used in this volume, or parts thereof, may not be reproduced in any
form without permission in writing from the Edgar Cayce Foundation,
Virginia Beach, Va.

The author and publisher also express their appreciation to the following for permission
to include the material indicated:

Pages 4 and 197, "Watching the Parade" (October 1969); "Native Sons, Daughters Mark History of Nation" (July 2, 1974). Reprinted by permission of the *Kentucky New Era.*

Pages 135 and 192, Table of Contents from *The New To-Morrow;* Diary Letter (May 14, 1947). Reprinted by courtesy of Association for Research & Enlightenment, Inc.

Page 138, "Spiritualistic Research Aim of New Atlantic University" (April 15, 1930). Reprinted by permission of *The Baltimore Sun.*

Page 148, "Court Frees Cayce, Reputed A 'Psychic.'" Copyright 1931 by The New York Times Company. Reprinted by permission.

Page 158, jacket back illustration from *My Years with Edgar Cayce* by Mary Ellen Carter, published by Harper & Row, Publishers, 1972. Reprinted by courtesy of the author and the Edgar Cayce Foundation.

Pages 166 and 174, frontispiece and title page from *There Is a River* by Thomas Sugrue. Copyright 1942, 1945 by Holt, Rinehart & Winston. Copyright © 1970 by Mary Ganey Sugrue. Copyright © 1973 by Patricia Sugrue Channon. Reprinted by permission of Holt, Rinehart & Winston, Publishers, and Curtis Brown Ltd.

Pages 171 and 172, illustrations from *Edgar Cayce, Man of Miracles* by Joseph Millard, published by Neville Spearman Ltd., London, 1961. Reprinted by courtesy of the publisher.

Library of Congress Cataloging in Publication Data

Cayce, Edgar, 1877–1945.
    Edgar Cayce's photographic legacy.
    Bibliography: p. xiii.
    1. Cayce, Edgar, 1877–1945.   I. Leary, David M.
II. Title.
BF1027.C3A54   133.8'092'4 [B]
ISBN: 0-385-12089-3
Library of Congress Catalog Card Number 76–23772
Copyright © 1978 by the Edgar Cayce Foundation
and David M. Leary
All Rights Reserved
Printed in the United States of America
First Edition

DEDICATION

This book commemorates all those dedicated individuals and groups, past and present, whose unwavering belief in the ideals and purposes of the Edgar Cayce readings have motivated their unselfish effort in helping seekers throughout the world avail themselves of this most priceless guidance.

It is also dedicated to the Cayce family and Gladys Davis Turner for their patience and tolerance of a relentlessly skeptical and frequently persecuting element (disbelieving medical profession, journalists, clergymen, attorneys, etc.) who dogged their widespread efforts of service and enlightenment to the thousands of ailing, crippled, and dying people, or those in need of spiritual guidance. Little different from public figures and prominent entertainers, their private lives seldom could be called their own, possibly due to some naivety out of their staunch faith in God and confidence in the Cayce psychic readings.

FOREWORD

Because of its unique design and in order for you to fully appreciate and understand the goals and purposes of this book, it is only fair to warn you that you should have already read, or should now take time to read, one or all of the following fine writings that cover practically all specifics of Edgar Cayce's life story *before* you delve into this photographic endeavor.

1. Thomas Sugrue's beautiful classic, *There Is a River.*
2. Gina Cerminara's great two, *Many Mansions* and *The World Within.*
3. Jess Stearn's stirring effort, *Edgar Cayce, the Sleeping Prophet.*

The purpose of this book, should you ask, is that of visual enhancement of all those mental pictures held in the minds of readers of the aforementioned books.

Should you, the reader, inadvertently find yourself pictured herein, yet incorrectly identified, or not identified at all, please accept this compiler's apology, and do inform me of your discovery so that corrections can be made in future printings. In some instances reliability of identification reverted back to the memory accuracy of contributors of their photographic material, for which I'm thankful all has been fairly uncomplicated. However, without Gladys Davis Turner's patience and fabulous memory, many identifications and very important details could not have been made.

PREFACE

During his forty-odd years photographing a great many people, coupled with clairvoyant or psychic dissertations, Edgar Cayce derived deep satisfaction through the intimacy afforded him by a rare combination of abilities. Needless to say, he loved people and literally worked himself to death serving his fellowman.

Despite the facts, *no* extensive files of Edgar Cayce's photographs and negatives exist today (a few glass-plate negatives were recently discovered in Hopkinsville, Kentucky). Numerous inquiries question this absence of pertinent material, even today. Most of us know, of course, that fires destroyed much of the earlier Cayce works. It is hoped, however, that more of his material will become available (possibly through the publication of this book) for future sequel publications or, at least, for the expansion of the existing exhibit in the A.R.E. (Association for Research and Enlightenment, Inc.) Headquarters, which will be completely reworked into back-lighted visuals, translucent photographic prints for the new A.R.E. Library/Conference Center.

As a professional photographer of many years standing, this compiler was equally distressed to discover how few of the existing available items were reproducible even with appreciable restoration efforts. It is suspected that there do exist many unrecognized excellent examples of Edgar Cayce's craftsmanship, possibly hung openly as family portraiture, stored away in attic trunks, boxes, or simply pasted into photo albums.

Toward the back of this book, special treatment has been given to a select few of Edgar Cayce's best achievements (available at this time). These outstanding photographic efforts indicate his ability to bring out a subject's true character and personality.

In the often frustrating process of finishing a particular project, such as you are about to scrutinize, I was faced with double-checking facts and faces. There were expected necessary corrections and changes after the Cayce family inspection and Gladys Davis Turner's eagle-eye shakedown, but it all came about quite smoothly, and most enjoyably, too. The final and "more authoritative" decisions were done in Nashville, Tennessee, through a personal visit with the grand lady of the Cayce family, Sarah Hesson, Edgar Cayce's youngest and only living sister.

After obtaining her permission to visit and forewarning her of our intentions, we chose a long five-day weekend to invade the Country Music Capital—that of September 12–16, 1974. Our Friday afternoon arrival reaped us a brief "coming home" welcome, some discussion of this book, and an eager acceptance of the original "manuscript" for a leisurely examination by Mrs. Hesson and her niece, "Sister" Mary's daughter Sarah Elizabeth (Mrs. Hesson's namesake). Her niece often came and spent much of Saturday and stayed overnight. In her excitement, Mrs. Hesson hoped to entice the younger woman to come over earlier, but she failed, and their double inspection took place as previously scheduled.

Another meeting Saturday afternoon gave us greater insight into the family life style—mostly during those early years, but including later and even more recent events involving these interesting younger nieces, nephews, and their children, who are already part of our everyday lives.

Our pre-arranged Sunday morning timing did not coincide with others' schedules, unfortunately, and we arrived just before church time, too late to meet Sarah Hesson's niece, who had made important identifications in a group picture and discovered a picture of her own mother that she had never before seen (a print of which she has now received for her very own). We retrieved my twelve-pound pictorial project, and after expressing our appreciation and farewells, we pointed our Gremlin back toward Virginia Beach, Virginia.

During the course of our conversations with this lovely lady, there emerged one profound observation from her that I must paraphrase for lack of an actual tape-recorded statement. She felt that this book will be indispensable to those who have acquainted themselves with the Edgar Cayce family, the psychic readings, and the organization derived from all this, but more especially the many devoted entities* involved in introducing the world to potentially improved ways of life found through use of this material. She envisioned great enthusiasm among those long-associated with "the work," particularly anyone who had readings from "Brother." Nostalgia won out in many instances and scenes herein were more than enough to bring tears to the eyes of Sarah Hesson and leave her in a momentary period of the "blues," to which she readily admitted without shame. We can't help but love this elegant woman's natural warmth, unmitigated honesty, and pure Southern hospitality. It was a memorable adventure we will cherish always.

It is our great hope that she will be as proud of the final published product as we are.

* Entity being a living person, whereas the Edgar Cayce psychic readings frequently used it to mean a particular individual receiving that specific reading.

ACKNOWLEDGMENTS

Gratitude is extended to those many contributors of photographic material over the years that comprise much of the background out of which this compilation began, as well as portions used in public relations exhibits and exclusive salon showings. We are especially grateful to those individuals who permitted the use of personal family pictures, their names, and their unsolicited testimonial letters. Especially without the many inspirational photographic gems Sally Cayce let me use from her prized collection, this publication's aura might have taken on an anemic hue. Love and thanks, Sally.

SUGGESTED READING MATERIAL

There Is a River, by Thomas Sugrue; Henry Holt & Company, 1942.

Many Mansions, by Gina Cerminara; William Sloane Associates, 1950.

The World Within, by Gina Cerminara; William Sloane Associates, 1957.

Edgar Cayce, the Sleeping Prophet, by Jess Stearn; Doubleday & Company, Inc., 1967.

The Outer Limits of Edgar Cayce's Power, by Edgar Evans Cayce and Hugh Lynn Cayce; Harper & Row Publishers, 1971.

My Life with Edgar Cayce, as told to Will Oursler by David E. Kahn; Doubleday & Company, Inc., 1970.

My Years with Edgar Cayce, The personal story of Gladys Davis Turner, by Mary Ellen Carter; Harper & Row Publishers, 1972.

Edgar Cayce, Man of Miracles, by Joseph Millard; Neville Spearman Limited, 1961.

A Search for God, Book I, and Book II, by Study Group One; Association for Research and Enlightenment, Inc., 1942.

Dreams, Your Magic Mirror, by Elsie Sechrist; Cowles Education Corporation, 1968.

Easy Does It, A program for better health and longer life, by Harold J. Reilly; Thomas Nelson & Sons, 1957.

Symbols and the Self, by Violet Shelley; booklet, A.R.E. Press, 1965.

A Prophet in His Own Country, by Jess Stearn; William Morrow & Company, Inc., 1974.

The Edgar Cayce Handbook for Health Through Drugless Therapy, by Harold J. Reilly and Ruth Hagy Brod; Macmillan Publishing Co., 1975.

CONTENTS

INTRODUCTION

Edgar Cayce would be pleased with this book. He worked as a photographer for many years in Bowling Green and Hopkinsville, Kentucky, and later in Selma, Alabama. Many of these pictures are his.

In thinking of my father as a photographer I remember him in three specific ways. He was excellent at taking pictures of children. While he was in Selma, Alabama, people brought their children to him from all over the state. He had the reputation as a photographer who could get a child to be natural. Later on I used to tease him a bit that he must have hypnotized the children in order to get them to pose so naturally for him. In Selma he taught me how to develop Kodak pictures and gave me a job of handling the Kodak business of the studio. At the time, it seemed quite an undertaking for me and I learned a great deal about picture developing and finishing from my father. Finally, I remember Dad as a photographer who began very early to try commercial work. I know that as far back as Bowling Green he used to pose me for advertisements that he sold to Mellon Foods. Later, I remember going with him and carrying the cameras when he photographed beautiful cotton plants and mechanical equipment in some of the industrial plants in Selma. Some of these pictures David Leary has included in this collection.

Many of the individuals who appear in this photographic historical record are people you will recognize by their names and activities in connection with the early years of Edgar Cayce's discovery of his ability—Dr. Wesley Ketchum, Dr. and Mrs. T. B. House, Carrie and Leslie Cayce, and many others—for they appear in *There Is a River* by Thomas Sugrue and *Edgar Cayce, Man of Miracles* by Joseph Millard, as well as many other books on Edgar Cayce.

The latter part of the book moves the Cayce family to Virginia Beach and includes photographs of the early construction of the hospital which operated for three years prior to the '29 stock market crash, which brought the close of the hospital as well as Atlantic University.

If you know anything about the Edgar Cayce story, I think you will find this book an exciting parallel that will bring many of the people and the scenes described in the books alive for you.

David Leary provides us with excellent commentary and a fine selection and arrangement of pictures—a photographic biography of Edgar Cayce.

HUGH LYNN CAYCE

EDGAR CAYCE'S
PHOTOGRAPHIC LEGACY

PHOTOS, NEWSCLIPPINGS, AND

PSYCHIC READINGS OF

EDGAR CAYCE

(Above) A photo of Edgar Cayce's mother. Our Lord's mysterious and wondrous ways brought Carrie Elizabeth Cayce's portrait (a slightly mutilated oval miniature) to my attention from its hiding place among mementos in her grandson's office (today's A.R.E. President, Hugh Lynn Cayce), after your compiler had resigned himself to the unhappy fact that there was no existing photograph from this period to accompany this one of the "Squire," Leslie B. Cayce, Edgar's father. No parents could have been more proud of a child than Carrie Elizabeth and the Squire, when their only son, ten-year-old Edgar, upon acceptance of their gift Bible, began studying it, reading it through several times that first year (twelve times by age twelve), and would continue to read it through every year of his life.

The only available photos of Sarah and Thomas Jefferson Cayce, Edgar's grandparents, which had to have been about 1865, the year when a photographer first settled in Hopkinsville. Even though Edgar idolized his grandfather, it was his grandmother who wouldn't allow him to be ashamed of his strange ability to see beyond mere physical density, auras, and angels (see *There Is a River,* by Thomas Sugrue, for details).

(Left and right) This early portrait of Edgar Cayce, probably taken by W. R. Bowles during Edgar's apprenticeship learning photography, was removed from its badly deteriorated background deliberately, out of frustration for finding no means to cure the situation. See for yourself. The same picture is at right with its original unretouched background (1899).

(Above) Not until his seventh year was Edgar Cayce exposed to book learning, which took place here in this little "red" schoolhouse near Liberty Church (probably a prominent crossroads south of Hopkinsville). Not to be confused with Beverly Academy, neither of which were public schools, certainly not in the sense of today's terminology, this was known as a subscription school. On the next page, with the photograph of Beverly Academy's school assemblage, Joe Dorris described this very thing in his "Watching The Parade" column (third paragraph) for Hopkinsville's New Era newspaper. Edgar's attendance here was of short duration, or so it seems, for he moved over to the Beverly Academy. The little schoolhouse still stands today on property acquired by William T. Turner, Hopkinsville's historian.

3

NEW ERA, Hopkinsville, Ky.
Early October 1969

"WATCHING THE PARADE"

By Joe Dorris

THIS IS EDGAR

The page 5 picture of Edgar Cayce and other pupils at old Beverly Academy, seven miles south of Hopkinsville on the LaFayette Road, was taken on Nov. 25, 1890.

Edgar was 10 years old at the time [actually, 13]. He had not yet attained clairvoyant fame.

Beverly Academy had been started only the year before as a subscription school, with parents paying to erect a building and hire a teacher so that their children might be able to attend school close to home. This was not an unusual practice in the era before the public school system got around to building schools all over the county.

Beverly later was taken into the county system. The old building is still standing but has been moved closer to Hopkinsville and set up on the property of William T. Turner, Christian County High teacher and well-known local historian.

Mr. Turner not only located the picture but succeeded in identifying most of the persons in the 79-year-old photo. . . .

The school stacked up as somewhat of a family affair, since there were 12 Cayces and 11 Majors in the picture. It is not known what kin some of the other Cayces are to Edgar.

One of the sisters, Miss Annie Cayce, later ran a millinery shop in Hopkinsville before moving to Nashville.

This school picture of Edgar is one of only two we have ever seen of the clairvoyant taken when he lived here. The other appeared in a special edition of the old Pembroke newspaper, for which Edgar, then in his early 20s, made the pictures.

The year is 1895 and Edgar's age 15 in this photo entitled: "A close friend, Ed Smith, and Edgar Cayce."

Compared to the school group to which young Edgar Cayce belonged, this baker's dozen is certainly outnumbered, but they look like an enthusiastic bunch. That's Gertrude Evans seated directly beneath that all-indicating arrow, knee-to-knee with the school "marm," who appears to be winking at the photographer, or perhaps she caught some dust in her eye.

A mere year or two later we find it's little Miss Glamour herself, head-to-head with her cousin, Edith Estella Smith, all gussied up for sport.

Truly the age of "available light photography," you fans of the current trend toward its use should greatly appreciate most of this book, but more especially the outdoor scenes and poses. Both modeling poses above are of twenty-year-old Gertrude Evans, rapidly becoming Edgar Cayce's number-one model (note the embossure directly above—"Photo by Cayce"). Gertrude, again at our bottom left with Edith Estella Smith seated beside her, Mary Cayce McPherson stands behind Gertrude next to Lillian Gray Salter, while Sarah Cayce peeks through from between broad hats, almost as though she wasn't supposed to be there.

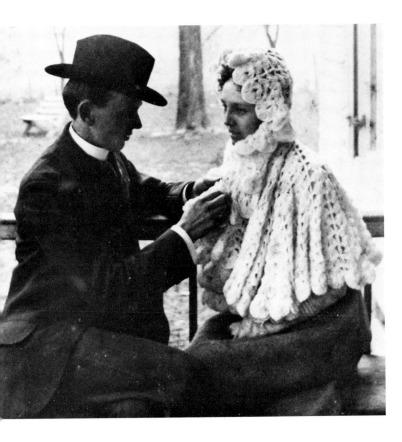

"Sure, honey, I do think knitting is creative, keeps you off the streets, gives us new sweaters all year long, allows us gifts for baby showers, anniversaries, and such, but how in the world did you get yourself knitted in without even an escapeway?" Can't you just imagine Edgar's concerned words to this lovely girl, the girl he has promised his love, to whom he is unofficially engaged, and it was more than likely far more serious than I've lead you to believe.

Whoever did the knitting, whether it was Gertrude Evans herself, a close friend, relative, etc., it was beautiful workmanship (no comment from the family), and Gertrude does look lovely and comfortable in the piece, especially in this "Whistler's Mother" pose. The goldfish are something else, an entirely different interest, and Gertrude certainly shows hypnotic interest.

Taking photographs, such as you find on these two pages, under the adverse conditions which these were shot, did take special talents, patience, and tenacity. This was a time before flash lamps (bulbs, if you wish) and floodlights were rare and very expensive, not to mention unreliable. Some of these interior poses have been trimmed because of their own shabbiness from deterioration. These are all Hopkinsville businesses.

The six interior photographs on this page and the previous one are from a set of glass negatives, all of which our hero, Edgar Cayce, made in Hopkinsville, Kentucky, a surviving few from what was estimated to be literally hundreds. The deterioration or separation of emulsion from the glass base (today, we call it film) can be seen across the tops of these two scenes and shows very black with white fringing. These old business establishments certainly had plenty of room in which to move about. The saloon above had space for several billiard tables.

This particular business was the Mammouth Clothing Company, its proprietor being J. E. Wall. Aside from this fact, ask your grandma what that white piece of women's apparel was used for, with those strange looking fingerlike protrusions at the bottom, the one tied to a display post at the far left side of the picture left. Did I hear the word corset? Did you notice that very few of the men above wore mustaches?

The above strangely posed photograph (no accompanying caption) defies logical explanation. What with Gertrude Evans almost a professional model, one might think it was a commercial picture, but what possibly could be the theme or product if it is an advertisement? Edgar must have used a long lens on his view camera, which causes the enlargement of people in the background.

"Let's get this showboat on the road" might fit the picture at left, in which (lower right corner) are Gertrude Evans and Edgar Cayce. Below, youthful Edgar has Smith cousins on either side and Gertrude's brothers behind him, looking as though the camera had interrupted them.

Flooding can happen almost any place that has rivers, but it usually requires the talents of an enterprising photographer to publicize them, like Edgar Cayce in Hopkinsville, November 1900.

The two lovely young ladies out for a mid-winter Sunday afternoon stroll (right) just happen to be Gertrude Evans and "Stella" (most handwritten captions make it look like "Stella" or "Steller," and it is actually Edith Estella Smith), possibly at the time of the flood pictures above.

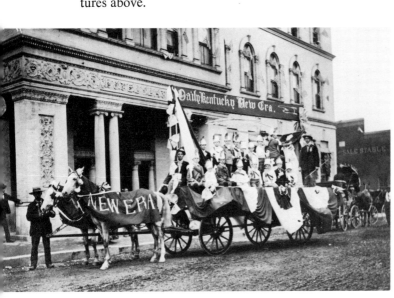

Stimulating is what best describes a parade, whether or not it is gigantic in scope or small in local carnival atmosphere, and that's what was behind the scene Edgar Cayce composed on film for us here (left), as well as the few following pages. In September 1900, this Elks parade entry paused in front of the Hotel Latham, a famous and elegant landmark until it burned down in 1941. This slight parade slowdown allowed young Cayce to record this fine memento of the time.

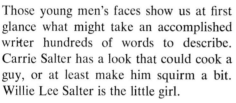

Those young men's faces show us at first glance what might take an accomplished writer hundreds of words to describe. Carrie Salter has a look that could cook a guy, or at least make him squirm a bit. Willie Lee Salter is the little girl.

(Top right) The elusive Mary Cayce was seldom photographed simply because she married young and moved to Nashville. This was enlarged from a miniature print, a snapshot. These other two pictures (below) are most likely from a series Edgar Cayce did on parades. I suspect the occasion is Memorial Day, Fourth of July, or similar national commemorative activity, and not necessarily related to the accompanying Buffalo Bill Shows parade. Some of these qualify for the salon section in this book and appear there also.

Scenes from the Buffalo Bill Shows parade series of pictures (October 1901). Edgar Cayce captured on film this high caliber parade about to begin its march from the heart of Hopkinsville north along Main Street.

I don't think I dreamed it, yet I thought there was a name for this Indian chief, who certainly seems to be an important element of the Buffalo Bill Shows. True, it was common practice for traveling shows to use Indian chiefs in their parades for authenticity and color. The photo below finds the band atop one of the animal wagons with quite a sidewalk following, and not just children.

This particular ornately decorated wagon, drawn by eight white horses and carrying five or more men on its top, could very well be for a tiger or a lion. The mounted riders following seem to be wearing metal helmets that reflect sunlight, but a strong magnifier doesn't identify them any better than that. However, the rider at far left front carries a U.S. flag.

The two boys are Porter (left) and Raymond Smith (I wonder if Ray got scolded for spreading his necktie as he did, which looks deliberate to me), while Ola Cayce and Estella Smith above and on the step below them Gertrude Evans (left) and Annie Cayce all posed very prim and proper for our hero.

Gertrude (left), Carrie (middle), and Estella probably wanted this to be different which explains the newspaper and alleged interest—or perhaps it was Edgar's idea since he took the photograph. It is out of the ordinary, and it was difficult to restore, too. No doubt both pictures were taken on location at "the hill," as were many throughout this book.

At right we have five of the same personalities from the top picture on the preceding page, but with the addition of Gertrude's two brothers, Lynn sporting a walking stick at left, and next to him Hugh preoccupied with some distraction out of the scene to our left.

For unusual innovations in picture taking, this has eye-catching appeal, even though it is out of focus. It was done by leaning a ladder up against a tree and endangering life and limb of seven people, four of whom had to help support each other. You know everybody here.

Through his affectionate embrace of Annie Cayce and Gertrude Evans, Raymond Smith also stabilizes his balance atop an orange crate.

It's more than just a possibility that Gertrude Evans is the girl in both pictures. They were actually side by side in an album belonging to her (we call your attention to the girl seated on the sunny slope beyond—left of the buggy and horse standing on the stream). The Smith brothers (not the cough-drop manufacturers) with Stella and Gertrude out in the woods at left below. Patience describes Ola Cayce (below right), posed for Edgar's camera, but it's not a choice location, even for his technique.

Can you find eight young people in the picture above left, taken at the entrance of an old mine?

The same foursome in the above two scenes sort of carried over from the previous page, while (below left) three women stand on the Cates Mill bridge. Three people in a two-horse carriage have just passed by.

On their way to Pilot Rock that looms above and behind them (left), no on-foot hike this, not judging by those buggy or surrey horses behind the same picnicking group below (if you look closely, carriage wheels are visible directly above Edgar Cayce's head). The caption merely states Gertrude and Edgar picnicking with friends on their way to the "rock." I suspect that Edgar Cayce had a self-timing device with which he accomplished these and the pictures that follow on the next few pages, otherwise how do you explain the same people in all photos? Someone who doesn't like having his or her picture taken is another possibility, but not probable (1901). From left to right: Mrs. Charles H. Hisgen, John Hisgen, Estella Smith, Alberta Hisgen, Sarah Dillman, Gertrude Evans, and Edgar Cayce.

Atop the "rock" sit Edgar and Gertrude (right), barely visible in the back-light flareover. Take note of the tripod-fitted folding box camera the man holds in center of photo. Then (below) we find our hero busily focusing his view camera beneath a black cloth (still a handy accessory with view cameras today), while the ladies appear disinterested. It was one of them though who shot this scene with the same camera called to your attention above (the lady all in black is missing).

Directly above, our hero is possibly stranded or thinks he has escaped from the group.

Most likely a different group, day, and location, but the Cayces are well represented. From left, two friends near Annie, W. A. McPherson sits in front of his bride-to-be, Mary (standing), yet another friend rests her hand on Ola's shoulder, next to Edgar and Gertrude Evans, while a friend sits behind Sarah in right front.

These charming cameo-type photos were in keeping with photographic styles of the times, and, in many circles, once again are considered stylish for certain poses.

Unfortunately, no cameo-type portrait was available of the Cayce's daughter, Mary, who was actually their third daughter in arrival. Annie, whom the whole family called "Sister," was the oldest of the four girls (lower left). Ola (upper left), second in age, was the family scholar. The youngest of Edgar's sisters, Sarah (directly above), lives today in Tennessee, paying her nephews and their families occasional visits.

His lack of formal education did not dampen Edgar Cayce's zest or enthusiasm to become the very best photographer he could. Even as an apprentice his enthusiasm led to photographic experimentation today regarded as routine procedure.

At some time in most young men's lives an unexplainable urge to grow hair on the face often produces either a mustache or beard, and, as in one case here, some will sport both. Mustached Edgar, at left, concentrates on his seated friend as a means of ignoring a possibly malfunctioning self-tripping camera device used to capture this interesting group and his own right profile.

One of Edgar Cayce's earlier photographic accomplishments (1903), this excellent family grouping is an achievement of real stature, especially considering he held their attentions directly on the camera throughout this time exposure. The "Leslie B. Cayce Family" is the title captioned to it, which didn't name the nieces and nephew seated down front, but Sarah Cayce is the third girl from left. Sitting

24

on chairs left to right, Gertrude Evans (we don't know if she had become Mrs. Edgar Cayce at this point), Carrie Elizabeth and Leslie B. Cayce, daughter Ola and another relative, Eltha Turner Minetree. Standing, left to right, a good friend Minnie Turner Knight (sister of Eltha Turner Minetree), Mary Cayce, Annie Cayce, and cousin Estella Smith. A baker's dozen and nobody moved!

These two lovely cameos are Christmas gifts that Gertrude and Edgar gave to each other on that festive occasion in 1900, about three years after the couple became engaged (by today's standards, that's unbelievable).

THE KENTUCKY NEW ERA

March 1901

Hopkinsville, Ky.

VOICE RESTORED

EDGAR CAYCE SUDDENLY RELIEVED OF A
TERRIBLE AFFLICTION.
VOCAL ORGANS PARALYZED A YEAR AGO
MADE WELL AS EVER.

On the night of April 18, 1900, young Edgar Cayce, a photographer in W. R. Bowles' gallery, suddenly lost his voice and for nearly ten months was unable to speak above a whisper.

Sunday night he recovered his voice as suddenly as he lost it. When he awoke Monday morning there was a feeling of relief about his throat and when he attempted to speak he saw that he could speak as distinctly as ever.

Overjoyed, the young man hastily dressed and rushed into his mother's room to break the good news. All day yesterday he was on the streets talking to his friends and receiving congratulations.

Mr. Cayce is a son of Mr. L. B. Cayce, and is a very worthy and deserving young man. When he became afflicted he was a salesman in a Main street store but had to give up this business and then secured a position with W. R. Bowles. His general health has continued good and he has worked regularly at his business.

It is supposed that his loss of speech was due to paralysis of the inferior muscles of the vocal organs. At times there was a stifling sensation about his throat and occasionally a little soreness. The feeling was akin to that felt by persons suffering from asthma and it was the absence of this feeling that first brought the realization of the good fortune that came to him while he slept.

Mr. Cayce during the last ten months had been under the treatment of specialists in this city, Nashville, Louisville, and Cincinnati all without benefit. Many other doctors had also looked into his case. It had been a month since he took any sort of medicine and his power of speech was restored as suddenly and unexpectedly as it was lost.

THE KENTUCKY NEW ERA

March 1901

Hopkinsville, Ky.

CAN TALK NOW

EDGAR CAYCE RECOVERS HIS VOICE.

RETURNED TO HIM AS SUDDENLY AS IT
LEFT HIM.

"I am the happiest man in Kentucky," said Edgar Cayce to the New Era this morning, and his tones proved his joy. Last night he could only speak in whispers. Today he talks as well as he ever could.

Lost Voice.

For ten long months his voice was lost. On the morning of the 18th of last April, Mr. Cayce, who was here from Louisville to visit his mother, started to answer some question she had asked him. His mind had formulated the reply, and his lips moved, but no word came from his mouth. He was practically dumb. The services of physicians and specialists were sought in vain. His vocal chords were paralyzed, they told him. He might some day recover his voice, but they could make no definite promise. He went to Louisville while Herman III, the noted magician, was there. To him young Cayce communicated his pitiable condition, and Herman hypnotized him.

While Hypnotized.

When in a mesmerized condition, Cayce, at the suggestion of the magician, was able to speak a few words, but on recovering his normal state, his voice was still gone. Returning to this city, he underwent a similar experience at the hypnotic suggestion of Mr. A. G. Layne, an amateur mesmerist of much skill.

But he made no progress towards regaining his voice. He continued under specialists until six weeks ago, when, having a slight attack of grip, he left off the treatment and had not since resumed it.

All Right Again.

He says he knew the moment he woke this morning he was all right again. He tried his voice and joyfully found he could speak. Then he hastened to acquaint the family with the good news. His many friends rejoice with him.

(Above) A few days prior to his twentieth birthday (1897) Edgar proposed marriage to Gertrude, who stalled him a whole week while she got family approval. (Right) Carrie Salter, a few years older, was more like a sister to Gertrude than an aunt. A professional buyer for a large department store, she was peacemaker in the large family of cousins.

(Below) Edgar seems rather bewildered that his father offered to trip his camera shutter, while (in back) Gertrude's young cousin, Raymond Smith, strikes the traditional male pose. That well-trimmed mustache and polished elegance to the right belongs to one Dr. Thomas Burr House, whom Carrie Salter would marry right after Gertrude and Edgar married (still several pages away). (Left) It appears that two young ladies have Edgar fenced in at "the hill."

Wedding photograph? If you're right, it's not the usual everyday run-of-the-mill
wedding pose. However, the gown our bride wears here looks like the one worn by
Gertrude in a bridal portrait (alone) which is devotedly displayed in Hugh Lynn
Cayce's office. So, after a courtship of six years, three months, and two days, Ger-
trude and Edgar were married June 17, 1903, in Hopkinsville. They went almost
immediately to a reception in the bride's honor a few miles away in Bowling Green,
Kentucky, where they were to make their home. Edgar was already employed by
L. D. Potter's Bookstore as a salesman (see *There Is a River* for further details).

NEW PARLOR GAME

EDGAR CAYCE, OF BOWLING GREEN,
SELLS INVENTION TO MFG. CO.

Mr. Edgar Cayce, head clerk in the bookstore of L. D. Potter & Co., on State street, is the author of a parlor game which will net him considerable money and bring him much fame. The name of the game is "The Pit," and is to be played with a deck of sixty-four cards. It is on the order of the famous game of "Bourse" but those who have played both games say that the one of which Mr. Cayce is the author is far superior to the other. The cards represent the various cereals, railroad, mining stock, etc., which are sold by the New York exchange. They are first dealt to the players and the object is to corner the market, on certain things. The one doing this is the winner. To play the game successfully requires considerable science and luck of course plays no small part. Mr. Cayce has sold his game outright to the Parker Manufacturing Co., of Salem, Mass. He received a good price for it and is naturally quite elated over its success. The game will be placed on the market as soon as a copywright can be procured.—
BOWLING GREEN NEWS

KENTUCKY NEW ERA

THE PIT

COPIES OF GAME INVENTED BY BOWLING
GREEN MAN RECEIVED HERE

Copies of "The Pit" or Board of Trade, the parlor game invented by Edgar Cayce of this city have been received by the Book Stores of Bowling Green and are in big demand. The game

is played with a deck of sixty-four cards and its object is to corner the market.

The people of Bowling Green have begun to play the game and it has already proven quite popular. The game is having a big run all over the United States.

TIMES JOURNAL
Bowling Green (Kentucky)
June 17, 1903

EDGAR CAYCE

TO BE MARRIED ON JUNE 17TH TO
MISS GERTRUDE EVANS, OF
HOPKINSVILLE.

Invitations are out to-day announcing the aproaching marriage of Edgar Cayce to Miss Gertrude Evans, of Hopkinsville. The wedding will occur on June 17th, at 4 o'clock p.m., at the home of the bride in Hopkinsville. There will be no attendants and the wedding will be a quiet home affair, and Mr. and Mrs. Cayce will come immediately to this city and take rooms with Mr. J. M. McClusky, on State street, where they will be at home to their friends.

Mr. Cayce is connected with the well-known book store of L. D. Potter & Co., coming here from Hopkinsville. He is a young man of perfect habits and the strictest integrity of character and by the manly manner in which he has conducted himself since his residence in this city has made himself hundreds of friends and is deservedly popular. He is one of our best known young business men and has the respect and esteem of all who know him.

Miss Evans is the attractive daughter of Mrs. Lizzie E. Evans, of Hopkinsville and is a social favorite in her home town. By her charming manners and sweet disposition she has endeared herself to all who know her and she will be given a cordial welcome to Bowling Green. The many friends of the parties will join the Times-Journal in advance of the happy event, in wishing them every happiness.

TIMES JOURNAL
Bowling Green (Kentucky)
June 17, 1903

CAYCE-EVANS

A pleasant surprise to society is the announcement of the marriage of Miss Gertrude Evans, of Hopkinsville, to Mr. Edgar Cayce, of this city. The marriage will occur at 4:30 p. m., June 17, at the home of the bride.

Three hundred invitations have been issued and the event will be one of great importance. The bride will be attired in a traveling gown, as they will leave immediately after the ceremony for this city. The ushers will be Messrs. Hugh and Lynn Evans, brothers of the bride and Dr. Hugh Beazley and R. H. Holland, of this city. There will be no lady attendants. The bride and groom will be at home to friends on lower State street after June 20.

Miss Evans is one of Hopkinsville's most popular young ladies and belongs to one of that city's best families. She is a young lady of many sweet traits and comes to us with the regrets of many friends at home. Mr. Cayce is the popular salesman at L. D. Porter's book store and is well know and liked by everybody. He has a fine disposition and is endowed with splendid business qualifications. His many friends here will be pleased to hear of his new relations and and extend to him their heartiest congratulations.

33

DR. J. R. PAINE'S RESIDENCE.

DR. R. D. MOORE'S RESIDENCE.

W. S. BUMPUS' RESIDENCE.

MRS. MATTIE GRAHAM'S RESIDENCE.

MRS. MAGGIE T. GARNETT'S RESIDENCE.

EDGAR A. HAIL'S RESIDENCE.

DR. T. P. ALLEN'S RESIDENCE.

W. H. JONES' RESIDENCE.

W. W. GARNETT'S RESIDENCE.

ANNOUNCEMENT.

By the issuance of this illustrated historical edition we desire to call the attention of the outside world to Pembroke in order that its advantages may be brought to the attention of the public. We are honestly convinced that Pembroke is one of the best towns of its size in the State, and if we can but carry this conviction to practical men of other sections we will have accomplished our primary purpose. The result which we hope this will produce is the ultimate purpose, viz.. the building up of the town. Pembroke desires and needs industries of all kinds. She will offer advantages and inducements. An experienced tobacco manufacturer, with some capital, can secure assistance here for the establishment of a large factory, and no enterprise would pay better. Here is a good opening for some live, experienced man to start the manufacture of plug, twist and smoking tobacco.

This book, then, is an invitation to men in all lines of business to investigate Pembroke's commercial advantages, and this invitation is most urgent to manufacturers.

We thank the business men and farmers for their liberal and hearty support, and for the interest they have manifested in its success.

We also desire to thank the contributors whose names appear with their articles for the favor which they have rendered this edition.

These are all photos by Edgar Cayce, used in a publication described in the Announcement.

Possibly a self-portrait, the newlyweds portrayed themselves in numerous character studies that can be identified as to time and place by their clothing, especially that of the bride. Hey, girls, how about that hat? It's not recommended for windy days.

Once more our setting is at "the hill," the Salter house in "Hoptown." We should entitle this, "The Cousins Four," what with the Evans brothers (Lynn at left and Hugh opposite) backed up by Raymond (left) and Porter Smith.

In the theater, taking the attention away from the star is called "upstaging," yet this looks as though Edgar deliberately featured the Squire in what appears to be self-inflicted portraiture. Do you suppose the Squire was embarrassed to see that pen and pencil standing at attention in his coat pocket after the printing was done?

That flaking sign implies that these five people made up the Edgar Cayce Art Company work force in Bowling Green, in 1906. Gertrude Evans Cayce sports a feather duster (you kids had best ask Grandma what that might be), while it's her brother, Lynn, with the tack hammer and glass sign. This restored Cayce original, a somewhat tattered horizontal, oval photograph looks quite good—except for the grayness and undetailed appearance of Mrs. Cayce's dress. Less than a year after this photo was taken, the Cayce studio and a large consignment of fine art (half their income) would be destroyed by fire.

(Left) Perhaps Edgar Cayce made some would-be humorous crack about Gertude's wild ostrich-plumed hat, and with her being pregnant, very sensitive, and with sympathetic brother Hugh present, it might explain the somberness here.

37

Lynn Evans

Hugh Evans

Namesake:
Hugh Lynn
Cayce, current
incarnation*
begun on
March 16, 1907.

(Above left) This portrait of Edgar was possibly self-inflicted (tripped the camera shutter remotely), or perhaps Gertrude did the honors. The restoration was laborious.

(Directly above) One of Edgar's earlier photographic manipulations, a double exposure printed on post-cards, done in good humor and quite novel to those who received the Cayce notes.

* The Cayce readings explain that every soul (while resting between lives) chooses to become human during many lifetimes in environments (in the Earth plane) suitable to its development, reincarnating until the record is flawless in God's eyes. Reincarnation came through Cayce in years following 1924 as "life readings," and it took many years for the Cayces to adjust to these concepts. An ancient Egyptian incarnation (e.g.) had the Cayces together then, too.

That is not an unfastened pant leg strap (Hugh's left leg), it's gouged film on the original negative.

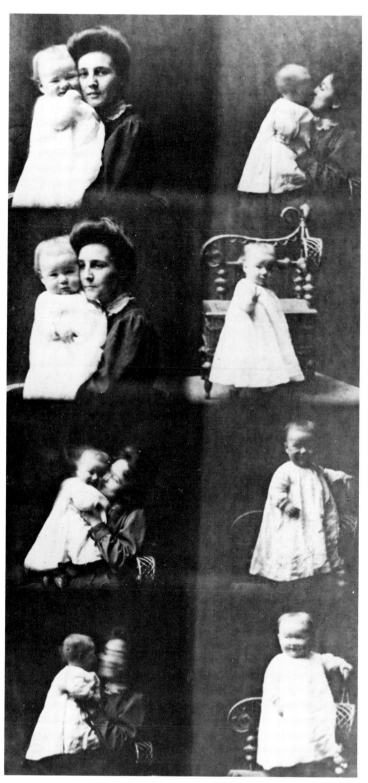

Someone is bound to criticize this choice because of numerous photographic faults, but I find it to be captivating, charming, and reflective of visual love natural to motherhood. I would venture to say that the father-photographer was trying out a sequence camera (in those days, a spring-activated camera, similar to early motion-picture equipment, was able to take rapid single exposures as fast as the shutter could be tripped), which accounts, in part, for blurred images and poor lighting conditions, in case you're at all interested in technical aspects of photography. This is undoubtedly late 1907.

Financially broke and discouraged from his seven years of ill-fated circumstances, yet not in debt, Edgar Cayce removed his photographic talents from Bowling Green, returned his young family to Hopkinsville, and is shown here just prior to his departure for employment in Alabama. Gertrude and Hugh Lynn (in his father's arms) would join him in a few weeks (see caption on page ii). With the exception of Edgar's mother, who seems oblivious to the pending departure, nobody appears overjoyed with the prospects, though the Squire has a look of detachment—or perhaps he's calculating time and travel distance necessary to visit the youngsters. Next to Gertrude stands Annie.

41

It's the quizzical expression that leads me to believe this was another self-portrait, despite the fact that Edgar was working for Tressler's Studios of Montgomery, Alabama, about this period. All evidence points to this as being the best portrait of Edgar Cayce in this book, but then you haven't seen the rest of them yet. It was found with long-forgotten stored items in Hopkinsville.

This charming photo of the lovely new mother, Gertrude Cayce, taken in Alabama about 1909, was copied, enlarged and restored from a miniature print. There is no doubt, at this point, who the photographer was . . . the most important man in her life. This is one of those expressions that defies description, but inspires attempting to caption it.

ILLITERATE MAN BECOMES A DOCTOR WHEN HYPNOTIZED

STRANGE POWER SHOWN BY EDGAR CAYCE PUZZLES PHYSICIANS

The medical fraternity of the country is taking a lively interest in the strange power said to be possessed by Edgar Cayce of Hopkinsville, Ky., to diagnose difficult diseases while in a semi-conscious state, though he has not the slightest knowledge of medicine when not in this condition.

During a visit to California last summer Dr. W. H. Ketchum, who was attending a meeting of the National Society of Homeopathic Physicians, had occasion to mention the young man's case and was invited to discuss it at a banquet attended by about thirty-five of the doctors of the Greek letter fraternity given at Pasadena.

Dr. Ketchum made a speech of considerable length, giving an explanation of the strange psychic powers manifested by Cayce during the last four years, during which time he has been more or less under his observation. This has attracted such widespread interest among . . . people, that one of the leading Boston medical men who heard his speech invited Dr. Ketchum to prepare a paper as part of the programme of the September meeting of the American Society of Clinical Research. Dr. Ketchum sent the paper, but did not go to Boston. The paper was read by Henry E. Harrower, M.D., of Chicago, a contributor to The Journal of the American Medical Association, published in Chicago. Its presentation created a sensation, and almost before Dr. Ketchum knew that the paper had been given to the press he was deluged with letters and telegrams inquiring about the strange case.

It is well enough to add that Dr. Wesley H. Ketchum is a reputable physician of high standing and successful practice in the homeopathic school of medicine. He possesses a classical education, is by nature of a scientific turn, and is a graduate of one of the leading medical institutions of the country. He is vouched for by orthodox physicians in both Kentucky and Ohio, in both of which states he is well known. In Hopkinsville, where his home is, no physician of any school stands higher, though he is still a young man on the shady side of Dr. Osler's deadline of 40.

Dr. Ketchum wishes it distinctly understood that his presentation of the subject is purely ethical, and that he attempts no explanation of what must be classed as mysterious mental phenomena.

Dr. Ketchum is not the only physician who has had opportunity to observe the workings of Mr. Cayce's subconscious mind. For nearly ten years his strange power has been known to local physicians of all the recognized schools. An explanation of the case is best understood from Dr. Ketchum's description in his paper read in Boston a few days ago, which follows:

"About four years ago I made the acquaintance of a young man 28 years old, who had the reputation of being a freak. They said he told wonderful truths while he was asleep. I, being interested, immediately began to investigate, and as I was 'from Missouri,' had to be shown.

"And truly, when it comes to anything psychical, every layman is a disbeliever from the start, and most of our chosen profession will not accept anything of a psychic nature, hypnotism, mesmerism, or what not, unless vouched for by some M.D. away up in the profession and one whose orthodox standing is unquestioned.

"My subject simply lies down and folds his arms, and by auto-suggestion goes to sleep. While in this sleep, which to all intents and purposes is a natural sleep, his objective mind is completely inactive and only his subjective is working.

"By suggestion he becomes unconscious to pain of any sort, and, strange to say, his best work is done when he is seemingly 'dead to the world.'

"I next give him the name of my subject and the exact location of same, and in a few minutes he begins to talk as clearly and distinctly as any one. He usually goes into minute detail in diagnosing a case, and especially if it be a very serious case.

"His language is usually of the best, and his psychologic terms and description of the nervous anatomy would do credit to any professor of nervous anatomy, and there is no faltering in his speech and all his statements are clear and concise. He handles the most complex "jaw breakers" with as much ease as any Boston physician, which to me is quite wonderful, in view of the fact that while in his normal state he is an illiterate man, especially along the line of medicine, surgery, or pharmacy, of which he knows nothing.

"After going into detail with a diagnosis and giving name, address, etiology, symptoms, diagnosis, and treatment of a case, he is awakened by the suggestion that he will see this person no more, and in a few minutes will be awake. Upon questioning him, he knows absolutely nothing that he said, or whose case he was talking about. I have used him in about 100 cases, and to date have never known of any error in diagnosis, except in two cases where he described a child in each case by the same name and who resided in the same house as the one wanted. He simply described the wrong person.

"Now this description, although rather short, is no myth, but a firm reality. The regular profession scoff at anything reliable coming from this source, because the majority of them are in the rut and have never taken to anything not strictly orthodox.

"The cases I have used him in have, in the main, been the rounds before coming to my attention, and in six important cases which had been diagnosed as strictly surgical he stated that no such condition existed, and outlined treatment which was followed with gratifying results in every case.

"One case, a little girl, daughter of a gentleman prominent in the American Book Company of Cincinnati, had been diagnosed by the best men in the Central States as incurable. One diagnosis from my man completely changed the situation, and within three months she was restored to perfect health, and is to this day.

"Now, in closing, you may ask why has a man with such powers not been before the public and received the indorsement of the profession, one and all, without fear or favor? I can truly answer by saying they are not ready to receive such as yet. Even Christ himself was rejected, for 'unless they see signs and wonders they will not believe.'

"I would appreciate the advice and suggestions of my co-workers in this broad field as to the best method of putting my man in the way of helping suffering humanity, and would be glad to have you send me the name and address of your most complex case and I will try to prove what I have endeavored to describe."

In further explanation, Dr. Ketchum gives this statement as obtained from the young man himself while asleep when asked to describe his own powers and the source of his mystifying knowledge:

"Our subject, while under auto-hypnosis, on one occasion, explained as follows:

"When asked to give the source of his knowledge, he being at this time in the sub-conscious state, he stated: 'Edgar Cayce's mind is amenable to suggestion, the same as all other sub-conscious minds, but in addition thereto it has the power to interpret to the objective mind of others what it acquires from the sub-conscious mind of other individuals of the same kind. The sub-conscious mind forgets nothing. The conscious mind receives the impression from without and transfers all thought to the sub-conscious, where it remains even though the conscious be destroyed.' He described himself as a third person, saying further that his sub-conscious mind is in direct communication with all other sub-conscious minds, and is capable of interpreting through his objective mind and imparting impressions received to other objective minds, gathering in this way all knowledge possessed by millions of other sub-conscious minds."

In all young Cayce has given more than 1,000 readings, but has never turned his wonderful powers to his pecuniary advantage, although many people have been restored to health by following out the course of treatment prescribed in his readings while in a state of hypnosis.

President James Hyslop of the American Psychic Society has made suggestions in regard to the development of the subject's powers. Other psychologists in Europe and America are seeking information, and Dr. Ketchum's plan is to have a committee of scientists of the highest standing come to Hopkinsville and investigate in a most rigid manner and make a report as to the truth of what is claimed, but not understood.

THE SEATTLE TIMES

PSYCHIC POWER NEW TO MEDICAL WORLD

SEATTLE TIMES
Hopkinsville, Ky., Saturday, Oct. 15 [1910].

The paper of Dr. W. H. Ketchum of this city which was read before the American Association for Clinical Research at Boston last week, in which he described the wonderful psychic power possessed by Edgar Cayce, a young photographer of this place in diagnosing diseases while under a self-imposed hypnotic spell, has caused wide discussion in medical circles throughout the country. Dr. Ketchum did not give the name of the young man in his paper, but as soon as people heard of it they recognized the description as being the work of Mr. Cayce, who has already achieved more than local fame thereby. Dr. Ketchum has known of Mr. Cayce and his work for more than two years and has had him diagnose nearly a hundred cases without a failure.

Others doctors readily testify to similar experience and others grudgingly admit there is something to it, but class it with quackery and refuse to give it their approval.

Mr. Cayce has been conscious of this particular power for about eight years and during that time has diagnosed probably a thousand cases, presenting all types of diseases. So far as these have been followed out he has never made a complete failure unless it came about through a confusion of names.

Method of Diagnosis

He will lie down on a bed or couch anywhere and by concentrating his mind produce a deep hypnotic sleep. When this condition is produced someone, generally his father, reads to him the name and address of the patient without further details as to such person or the disease. Many times Cayce has gone into the spell without any idea as to the patients or where they live. In a few seconds he begins talking and in a clear, positive tone tells to the minutest detail the trouble with the person, his remarks being recorded by a stenographer.

He is entirely without medical education yet he describes the most complicated organs of the body, the nervous system, the circulation, always telling the exact physiological designation. Yet when awakened he is amazed at the long and difficult words he has used and laughingly professes his ignorance of how they are spelled or what they mean. Awake he knows absolutely nothing about anatomy or diseases.

Recently he diagnosed the case of a young woman in Cleveland. The day before the transcript of the reading reached Cleveland an operation was performed on the patient and the surgeon wrote verifying the correctness of Mr. Cayce's diagnosis.

The case of a woman who lived in Chicago was submitted to him, and as soon as he began to talk under the spell Cayce became much excited and stated that the woman was bleeding to death internally as the result of an operation and that unless prompt measures were resorted to she would die. The transcript was hastened to Chicago but before it arrived the woman died exactly as Cayce had predicted she would.

Cayce will not disclose names of his patients for newspaper use, but is always willing to submit them or himself to doctors for investigation. He is 31 years of age. He uses his power only when called upon and taking such remuneration as is given him.

Dr. Ketchum has implicit faith in him and has done all he can to attract the attention of the progressive medical profession to the work. Even Cayce says he does not know just what he can do. He lives here with his father, L. B. Cayce, an insurance man. He is married and has one child.

THE NEW YORK TIMES

PSYCHIC POWER NEW TO MEDICAL WORLD

Hopkinsville, Ky., Saturday, Oct. 15 [1910].

The paper of Dr. W. H. Ketchum of this city which was read before the American Association for Clinical Research at Boston last week, in which he described the wonderful psychic power possessed by Edgar Cayce, a young photographer of this place in diagnosing diseases while under a self imposed hypnotic spell has caused wide discussion in medical circles throughout the country. Dr. Ketchum did not give the name of the young man in his paper, but as soon as people heard of it they readily recognized the description as being the work of Mr. Cayce, who has already achieved more than local fame thereby. Dr. Ketchum has known of Mr. Cayce and his work for more than two years and has had him diagnose nearly a hundred cases without a failure.

Others doctors readily testify to similar experiences and others grudgingly admit there is something to it, but class it with quackery, and refuse to give it their approval.

Mr. Cayce has been conscious of his peculiar power for about eight years and during that time has diagnosed probably a thousand cases presenting all types of disease. So far as these have been followed out he has never made a complete failure unless it came about through a confusion of names.

Method of Diagnosis

He will lie down on a bed or couch anywhere and by concentrating his mind produce a deep hypnotic sleep. When this condition is produced some one, generally his father, reads to him the name and address of the patient without further details as to such person or the disease. Many times Cayce has gone into the spell without any idea as to the patients or where they live. In a few seconds he begins talking and in a clear, positive tone tells to the minutest detail the trouble with the person, his remarks being recorded by a stenographer.

He is entirely without medical education, yet he describes the most complicated organs of the body, the nervous system, the circulation, always telling the exact physiological designation. Yet when he is awakened he is amazed at the long and difficult words he has used and laughingly professes his ignorance of how they are spelled or what they mean. Awake he knows absolutely nothing about anatomy or diseases.

Recently he diagnosed the case of a young woman in Cleveland. The day before the transcript of the reading reached Cleveland an operation was performed on the patient and the surgeon wrote verifying the correctness of Mr. Cayce's diagnosis.

The case of a woman who lived in Chicago was submitted to him, and as soon as he began to talk under the spell Cayce became much excited and stated that the woman was bleeding to death internally as the result of an operation and that unless prompt measures were resorted to she would die. The trnscript was hastened to Chicago, but before it arrived the woman died exactly as Cayce had predicted she would.

Cayce will not disclose names of his patients for newspaper use but is always willing to submit them or himself to doctors for investigation. He is 31 years of age. He uses his power only when called upon and taking such remuneration as is given him.

Dr. Ketchum has implicit faith in him and has done all he can to attract the attention of the progressive medical profession to the work. Even Cayce says he does not know just what the power is, but he knows what he can do. He lives here with his father, L. B. Cayce, an insurance man. He is married and has one child.

THE KENTUCKY NEW ERA

Oct. 15, 1910

MR. CAYCE TO OPEN STUDIO

PHOTOGRAPHER AND PSYCHIC
DIAGOSTICIAN LOCATES HERE
IN CONNECTION WITH HIS GALLERY HE
WILL EXERCISE HIS POWER
FOR BENEFIT OF SICK.

Edgar Cayce, the psychic diagnostician about whom so much has appeared in print lately has arranged to open a photographic studio on Main street. His equipment is now in transit and he expects to get the studio open this week. It will be one of the most complete enterprises of the kind in this part of the state, and will occupy the offices recently occupied by Judge A. H. Anderson during the taking of the census and the operating room will be the large quarters on the same floor formerly occupied by Miss El Blumensteil.

Since his psychic power has become so widely advertised Mr. Cayce has been overwhelmed with applications from people who desire him to examine their cases and he will do a good deal of this work in connection with his studio.

THE CINCINNATI TIMES-STAR

Oct. 10, 1910

MAN'S STRANGE POWER PUZZLING PHYSICIAN

WHILE IN HYPNOTIC SLEEP EDGAR CAYCE,
KENTUCKY PHOTOGRAPHER, DIAGNOSES
COMPLICATED DISEASES ACCURATELY.

Edward Cayce of Hopkinsville, Ky., while in sleep, induced by auto-suggestion, diagnoses complicated diseases with such accuracy that physicians, who are investigating his strange power, are able to offer no explanation. Cayce is a photographer. He is thirty-two years old and a son of L. B. Cayce. Eight years ago he was hypnotized by a showman, and while in a trance told how he should be treated for vocal paralysis, from which he was suffering. His voice was quickly restored. Since then he has experimented widely with remarkable success. While in hypnotic sleep, when the name and location of a person is given him, he rapidly and clearly describes any disease and uses medical terms and phrases with ease and assurance, which he is unable to pro-

47

nounce when awake. Normally he knows nothing whatever of physiology, anatomy or materia medica. Cayce's mysterious power was made the subject of a paper by Dr. W. H. Ketchum of Hopkinsville, Ky., which was read before the American Association of Clinical Research in Boston. Dr. Ketchum says that in more than one hundred cases which he has submitted to Cayce, he had never failed to describe perfectly the condition of the patient, except in two instances, when he was confused by similarity of names. Cayce has never used his strange gift to make money. He makes a good living as a photographer and says he knows nothing of what he says while in a trance. A number of eminent psychologists are showing an interest in the case.

THE CHICAGO EXAMINER
February 19, 1911

PSYCHIST DIAGNOSES AND CURES PATIENTS

IGNORANT OF MEDICINE, TURNS HEALER
IN TRANCE
KENTUCKIAN NEW PUZZLE FOR
PHYSICIANS.
ADMITS HE CAN REMEMBER NOTHING
THAT OCCURS IN
HYPNOTIC SLEEP.
SOLVES MURDER MYSTERY
REMARKABLE AND SUCCESSFUL
TREATMENTS ARE SWORN
TO IN AFFIDAVITS.

by Roswell Field.

Hopkinsville, Ky., Feb. 18
"You have before you Mr. August Boehme of 632 Overton Street, Newport, Ky.. Go over him carefully, examine him thoroughly and tell us what his condition is now."

So spoke the "suggester," the father of Edgar Cayce, Jr., the auto-hypnotist, or psychic diagnostician, to the man lying in

48

a trance before him. Very slowly came the reply from the sleeping body.

"Mr. August Boehme of 632 Overton Street, Newport, Ky.. Yes, we have him here. We have had him before. His condition here is much improved along the circulation, through the digestion, etc., etc."

But I am beginnning at the wrong end of the story. Who is Edgar Cayce, Jr., and why should he, in a hypnotic condition, be interrogated as to the unseen Mr. Boehme of Newport? That is the question that is exciting the people of his town, perturbing the doctors and delighting the spiritualists, the psychologists and all other seekers after the truth if truth there is in the occult.

Tobacco War at Hopkinsville

Far back in the mental recesses there is a lurking memory of Hopkinsville as once a center of sensations in which the famous Joe Mulhatton figured. There is a haunting recollection that in this pretty town first appeared the only original seven-legged calf, together with other prizes, the delight of Mr. Barnum's professional life.

There was a genuine sensation two years ago when the Night Riders swooped down on the town and suburbs, for Hopkinsville is the heart of a great tobacco raising country, and the tobacco war is a distinct part of martial history. But all these manifestations, great or trivial, have not the flavor of mystery and amazement caused by Edgar Cayce, Jr., farmer's son, photographer and psychic diagnostician.

THE CHICAGO EXAMINER
Oct. 15, 1910

And I am going to tell you his story as nearly as possible as he told it to me.

Near the end of Main street in Hopkinsville, at the side of a narrow flight of stairs is the sign, "Cayce Studio." At the head of the stairs are two doors, one of them leading directly into a photograph establishment, the other indicating a suite of rooms on the glass entrance of which is painted "Edgar Cayce, Jr., Psychic Diagnostician." Known then at the outset that the photographer and the psychic gentleman are identical.

Possessed Psychic Powers

Locally for six or seven years, more or less nationally for perhaps four or five months, the fame of Edgar Cayce has been extending. It was rumored that although a simple, easy going modest young man, with very little education, he possessed marvelous psychic powers. He was enabled to demonstrate that while in a trance, a cataleptic state, or whatever you may choose to call it, he departed from himself, became seemingly another person, could bring before his mental vision people a hundred, a thousand, three thousand miles away, and without the slightest previous knowledge of their physical condition, diagnose their cases and prescribe treatment for their ailments as his extraordinary mental sight directed.

More than this, he would talk in the parlance of the medical profession, discourse with a marvelous knowledge of anatomy and physiology, and make his diagnoses with extraordinary quickness and accuracy.

When the doctors at the homes of the patients made their own diagnoses they were compelled to admit that Cayce had not merely corroborated their own conclusions, but had given suggestions which had escaped them.

Called a Fake by Doctors

Doctors are a very ethical lot of gentlemen, and do not approve of such dabbling with the black art. So many of them, while openly wondering, declared that Cayce was a fake—but how and where? To conclude this imperfect introduction it is necessary to say that when Cayce came out of his trance he was neither doctor nor diagnostician; he was merely a simple farmer's boy, a photographer, if you please, who wouldn't know a solar plexus nerve from a capillary circulation. He says so himself, and I take his word for it cheerfully.

As I was only mildly interested in the photographer, but much so in the psychical gentleman, I turned from the studio and sought the diagnostician. I found him with his father sitting in a reception room, apparently "killing time" in the most approved Kentucky fashion. His appearance was neither conspicuously encouraging nor disappointing. His photograph, which is an admirable one, bears out the impression of a tall, slender young man, with good, honest eyes, sufficiently wide apart, a high forehead and just the ordinary features.

He admitted that he is thirty-three years of age, though he does not look over twenty-five, and he told me how the Cayces came from France many years ago, and how one of his grandfathers married an Irish girl, thus showing the possible confusion of Cayce and Casey, . . . [continued in original].

49

CAN SEE DISEASE WHILE IN TRANCE

PHYSICIAN SAYS KENTUCKY MAN HAS WONDERFUL POWERS.

WITHOUT EDUCATION
TRIAL IN 1,000 CASES PROVES ABILITY TO DIAGNOSE, HOWEVER

Hopkinsville, Ky., Oct. 15. (Special.)

The paper of Dr. W. H. Ketchum of this city which was read before the American Association for Clinical Research at Boston last week, in which he described the wonderful psychic power possessed by Edgar Cayce, a young photographer of this place, in diagnosing diseases, while under a self imposed hypnotic spell, has caused wide discussion throughout the country.

Dr. Ketchum did not give the name of the young man in his paper, but as soon as people heard of it they readily recognized the description as being the work of Mr. Cayce, who has already achieved more than local fame thereby. Dr.

Ketchum has known of Mr. Cayce and his work for more than two years, and has had him diagnose nearly a hundred cases without a failure.

Other doctors readily testify to similar experiences and others grudgingly admit there is something to it, but class it with quackery and refuse to give it approval.

Has Diagnosed 1,000 Cases.

Mr. Cayce has been conscious of his peculiar power for about eight years, and during that time has diagnosed probably a thousand cases, presenting all types of disease. So far as these have been fol-

lowed out he has never made a complete failure unless it came about through a confusion of names. Mr. Cayce works in this way:

He will lie down on a bed or couch anywhere and by concentrating his mind produce a deep hypnotic sleep. When this condition is produced some one, generally his father, reads to him the name and address of the patient without further details as to such person or the disease. Many times Mr. Cayce has gone into the spell without any idea as to the patients or where they live. In a few seconds he begins talking, and in a clear positive tone tells to the minutest detail the trouble with the person, his remarks being recorded by a stenographer.

Without Medical Education.

He is entirely without medical education, yet he describes the most complicated organs of the body, the nervous system, the circulation, etc., always using the exact physiological designation. Yet when he is awakened he is amazed at the long and difficult words he has used and laughingly professes his ignorance of how they are spelled or what they mean. Awake he knows absolutely nothing about anatomy or diseases.

Recently he diagnosed the case of a young woman in Cleveland. The day before the transcript of the reading reached Cleveland an operation was performed on the patient and the surgeon wrote verifying the correctness of Mr. Cayce's diagnosis.

The case of a woman who lived in Chicago was submitted to him, and as soon as he began to talk under the spell Mr. Cayce became much excited and stated that the woman was bleeding to death internally as the result of an operation, and that unless prompt measures were resorted to she would die. The transcript was hastened to Chicago, but before it arrived the woman died exactly as Mr. Cayce had predicted.

Willing to be Investigated.

Mr. Cayce will not disclose names of his patients for publication, but is always willing to submit them or himself to doctors for investigation. He is 31 years of age.

Dr. Ketchum has implicit faith in him and has done all he can to attract the attention of the progressive medical profession to the work. Even Mr. Cayce says he does not know just what the power is, but he knows what he can do. He lives here with his father, L. B. Cayce, an insurance man. He is married and has one child.

While working for the Tressler Studios, this fine photographic effort was recorded for posterity, but mainly for the Cayce families. When newspapers were given Dr. Wesley H. Ketchum's version of the Edgar Cayce story (which was done without Edgar's knowledge or consent), unscrupulous reporters stole Edgar's portraits right off the Squire's wall, including this particular pose. The portrait I copied for this print displayed the message shown on page 53 , which has been verified as the actual handwriting of Dr. Ketchum. Nevertheless, because of the national notoriety and visible and audible gossip, etc., Ketchum convinced Edgar to come back and work with him in Hopkinsville again during 1911. It was a short-lived venture that sent Edgar back to Selma angry and disgusted (see *There Is a River* for details).

Edgar Cayce, the
Wonder Psychic of
the 20th Century.
Brought to the attention
of the world by yours
very truly—
Wesley H. Ketchum.

This is not the same photograph used in
the national newspaper coverage. From
the newspaper clippings I have viewed,
they all used one pose, which was a left
profile of Dr. Wesley H. Ketchum.

Although the newspaper articles are already included in this book, these and other reference notations were left in the contents of some Cayce readings to benefit you individuals who would seriously make the effort to search out and at least read this engrossing additional material.

Background: See 294-1 and 294-2 re. EC's early work. Also see 10/9/10 **254-1**
N.Y. Times, 2/19/11 Chicago Examiner re. EC's gift.

This psychic reading given by Edgar Cayce at Hopkinsville, Kentucky, this 13th day of February, 1911, on the work of Edgar Cayce.

P R E S E N T

Edgar Cayce; L. B. Cayce, Conductor; Katherine Faxon, Steno.

R E A D I N G

Edgar Cayce—Jr.

Time of Reading   *Hopkinsville,*
4:15 P.M.   *Kentucky*

LBC: *You have before you Edgar Cayce, Jr., self.*

EC: *Edgar Cayce, Jr.? Yes, we have had him here before.* **[GD's note:** His uncle was named Edgar Cayce.]

LBC: *Now, he, in his subconscious mind, has wonderful powers. We are about to enter into a great business and professional enterprise, and if he is properly managed, will make a success for himself and others associated with him. We want you to outline a mode of procedure that will be successful. We want you to tell us how to organize.*

EC: *Subconscious self, Edgar Cayce, Jr.? We have the subconscious self of Edgar Cayce, which partakes, or is amenable to suggestions from the control, and in a subconscious state.*

We organize for a great business; we have it, a business from different standpoints. We have a difference from the capabilities of his work; we have it from the power of the work. We can follow it from one field, or the other field. We can take it from the material, from the spiritual, or we can take it from the ethereal. It can be treated from either. We have it from either point, but we cannot mix the points. Same as we have in the body, physical, mental and abnormal or spiritual self. We have the use of all in the physical body, same as we have the use of all in the material world.

We organize a business venture.

Q-1. Where should we locate?

A-1. We have in the body now, a mind, a physical body, and the mental self of Edgar Cayce, Jr., as we have it here in the material world. We have now, its relations between the material world, or business world, and we have its relations between the mental or spiritual world—the mental self, the action from other bodies of the same material world. We have the action of consequent control through the ethereal world. We have an organization of the materialistic through bodies outside, controlling the portions or workings through the business of the works done by this ethereal body here of Edgar Cayce.

We have into the world all bodies subject to ethereal control. We have all bodies subject to (that is, the abnormal mind, now) ethereal control. Subject to

54

ual has this in itself. The condition that we have to help the individual bodies, are through their individual self, assisted by material objects obtained into the mental mind of the material man.

   We have this body here, this mind, this matter that we have here, of Edgar Cayce, Jr., through the ethereal world, as it gathers from the force given out either from the present, the past, and given back to the material man through the subconscious self, acting in the material body, by the control, to which it is in a state of coma too.

   The control of the subject of self first is to be gained and kept under control—the best control of the body in itself.

   We have first the direction to the body, wherein we have communication, or communion with the control, we have gained to the ethereal world, that is, outside, the minds of all matter. It is the mental capacity of all matter. All mental man, through the control by suggestion to the mental, or the invisible action of matter on the mind in the individual itself, or the organism of the system wherein the man is made. The development of each is to be gained by its control, which is gained by its material work shown to the material man. That is, we have here man (that is, humanity) by nature, handed down from one body to the other, looks for material, or acts on the physical self, and action gained from the ethereal, or mental, without its production through the material has no effect on the man.

   The place where we use these, for this, is anywhere, so we have it fixed for use to develop or show to the mental, physical man, the structure of things gained through the channel, where we have contact here with the material world, and the means whereby these can be gained is from the ones that see personal gain to self.

Q-2.   Where and how should we obtain the necessary money for this business?

   A-2.   Where and how should we obtain the necessary money for this business? That depends on the place and business we have had here before. Now, we have a business here within this body. We have the materialistic, we have the physical and we have the mental.

Q-3.   We want the business of diagnosing the physical condition of bodies.

   A-3.   Physical condition of bodies? diagnosing the mental condition, physical condition, the abnormal condition of other bodies? The physical body, acted on by physical means, material means, for physical benefits for individual bodies?

   The action of material things to individual bodies, claim to the individual body, a thoroughness of the material thing in itself. Whereby, or how, shall we gain the material means for the furtherance of the ethereal project here?

Q-4.   Well, tell us where and by what means to get this money.

   A-4.   Only whereby they receive personal gain, or physical gain, gain for the material man or body, in the outside world—as we have it here at present. Where we have established in itself, whereby it is shown to the material world the workings of the ethereal body, do we establish credence with the material. Thereby, we gain credence of the material body, and they give of their means for personal gain. As we give credence to these, and it is shown by its material gain through the mental, physical man, or to the material man, he will give of his means for the maintenance of the concourse through the ethereal and physical man.

Q-5.   How shall the professional side be arranged and managed so as to obtain the greatest success?

   A-5.   By doing these things giving to the material man from the ethereal world here. Here, you see, we have communication from all of these, from before. We have communication from all these present, and from the physical bodies. The physical condition of a body is the condition existing in that body at the present. If we have a physical body suffering from a mental state; from a physical state or from an abnormal condition of all combined together, it is given from the ethereal state by that condition whereby we show to the mental man outside, or the material man, whereby we gain credence from these; whereby we are able to show ourselves to the man here, and the closer we are followed here with these, the stronger we become, because we become more thorough, you see, in our works. We show more strongly to the material man the workings of the ethereal world. As we gain more control to these, we gain more to the abnormal or subconscious mind of man, to give credence to these conditions that exist in all bodies. Whereby we gain these controls is got by how these are to be given out to individual selves, as we have now, here.

This body, which has become racked with pain, you see, from the physical condition of the man—if we give this then to the material man, as through this agent here, we rid this body of this pain. The material man becomes conscious of this body because we have had material good to the man. We answer both to his inner conscience and to the physical man, and to the outside world, whereby we gain credence—whereby the material that has been used into this man, or has used these agencies for this man here, gains credence, and the minute we gain credence and give credit to ourselves, we lose it all.

(10/15/50 issue of THE SEARCHLIGHT, "Chronology of the Life and Work of Edgar Cayce and the A.R.E.," gives brief of main events in Edgar Cayce's life prior to the readings which are in A.R.E. files.) [See a copy of it under 254-1 Supplement.]

(Left) Gertrude holds Hugh Lynn force-ably from dashing away and seemingly comforts his playmate long enough for the picture-taking procedures. (Below) Behind Estella Smith (left front) sits her would-be twin, despite contradiction, name, or verification. Elizabeth Salter Evans sits behind her "baby" sister Carrie Salter House, and leans away from Estella's gentleman friend, Ed Smith (no relation). Take note, ladies, of those hats of fashion loaded with artificial fruit . . . wow!

(Below) Edgar seems determined to make a cowboy out of young Gray Salter through this very direct introduction to an equally young heifer.

(Above) Hugh Lynn had already begun his modeling career. This could have been a commercial photograph, too, but the boy acts as though the burro and outfit are his.

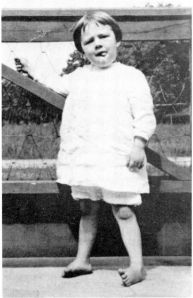

Not the least bit camera shy and looking like a used-car salesman, especially in the lower pose, Hugh Lynn Cayce seems as though he is checking his car out after the two prospects (above) have test-driven it.

Puzzled Tommy House is probably trying to figure out how to comply to Edgar's "smile for the camera" with his mouth full of watermelon and seeds.

(Below) Now, it's Hugh Lynn's turn to be caught with a mouthful of melon seeds. S'pose he was aware that his watermelon slice had the pigtail stem still attached? Kids don't change much, do they, when it comes to clothes, etiquette, and eating?

Because of his great interest in the Bible and spiritual guidance, Edgar and Gertrude almost immediately became active in church functions...above, he is surrounded by his Sunday school class in Selma's First Christian Church (1912).

Wood Gray

Dick Dickerson

Alf Butler

Edgar Cayce

Harry Bredin

Possessing a remarkable sense of humor, Edgar Cayce is shown in these two scenes with the First Christian Church "Helping Hands" ladies group. They were able to talk him into acting in some of their church plays, even though here they were only on a picnic and he was merely cutting up. As in the picture at left, the girl in "sailor" attire is Mamie Gray, who (above) rests her arm across a friend's knees. Agnes Priester is at far right sitting with sprig of flowers in lap. Edgar's "fetching" bonnet (above) belongs to the young lady directly in front of him. She is shown wearing it at left. Sorry, but these are the only identifications we could make, even though some of the same faces appear in the small "outing" shot atop the next page.

The caption on the back of the photo read: "We're out for a good time." Same church group on a different picnic in Selma's Elkdale Park. Restoration of the photo was almost impossible, and where cellophane tape was used to patch rips you can readily see retouching efforts. Edgar evidently set up the camera for someone else to trip (he's about center in the back row). Flash powder was always sheer guesswork.

I asked the roses as they grew
Richer and lovelier in their
hue
What made their tints so rich
and bright,
They answered—
Looking toward the Light—

Above is poetry by Edgar in his *almost* legible handwriting, which appeared on a postcard with the Cayce family picture. It was snapped by Ruth or Dick Dickerson, who appear twice in the photos at center right and lower right. Clothing differences indicate our camera shoot-out wasn't all on the same day. Hugh Lynn must have sold his parents on knickers above the knees as being fashionable.

The late afternoon sun directly in a person's eyes is no way to get their best personality, not even Carrie Elizabeth Cayce (Edgar's mother), standing at the left of these fence sitters. Next to her is Mamie Gray, who took the lower picture so Gertrude could be in it, as Gertrude did this one. Then, we have Dick and Ruth Dickerson, with Edgar hiding under what appears to be a new hat. Below, they all found one of Elkdale Park's benches by a pond or stream, but nobody, except Carrie Elizabeth, seems able to look up full face. This was her first visit to Selma.

Lest the reader be confused by the name "Dallas" (below), it is the name of the county in which this church was located. The sign relates to a membership drive competition with a First Christian Church in another Alabama county.

(Left) The First Christian Church Sunday school group, which gained some fame as the Seven Class, published a weekly paper called *Sevenette* (see a sample on the next page), which was widely distributed to and read by the general public throughout the Selma area. Young people came from far and wide to join this remarkable Sunday school class mainly because of its resourceful teacher, Edgar Cayce, shown in front row, second from right.

(Left) No, kids, those are "only a bunch of daisies" that Dickerson and Cayce are picking for the ladies pictured on the previous page. (Below left) It looks like a Miami Beach dude, but it's Edgar on postcards again, without further info. (Below) A sweet young thing from a church play, no doubt.

So then because thou art Lukewarm and neither cold nor hot. I will spue the out my mouth.

The Sevenette

PUBLISHED BY CLASS NO. 7

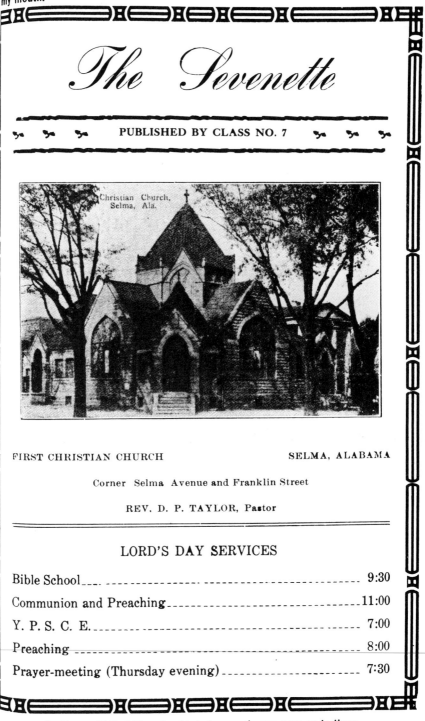

FIRST CHRISTIAN CHURCH   SELMA, ALABAMA

Corner Selma Avenue and Franklin Street

REV. D. P. TAYLOR, Pastor

LORD'S DAY SERVICES

Bible School _____ 9:30

Communion and Preaching _____ 11:00

Y. P. S. C. E. _____ 7:00

Preaching _____ 8:00

Prayer-meeting (Thursday evening) _____ 7:30

As Ye would that Men should do to you, do yea even so to them

These pages are samplings copied from Edgar Cayce's collection of the publication his famous Sunday school Seven Class produced weekly for almost two years. They were written and put together by Edgar, advertising appeared in them and paid for printing, and Hugh Lynn Cayce delivered copies to merchants around town on Saturday afternoons.

With this issue The Sevenette reaches its first Mile stone, and while it has not always been easy to obtain matter for the sheet, if we have made one smile, one thought of ones duty to their God and Savior, one more incentive to do more for ones fellow man, our years work has not been in vain.

We feel rather proud that others have followed our lead, and are issuing similar papers.

We have had repeated calls from various parts of the country for copies of the paper.

To our advertisers, who have helped make the Sevenette possible we extend our thanks.

We believe in The Sevenette and the principals it stands for, and the place such a paper should hold among its readers and trust it will have many more years of SERVICE.

7-------------------- ---------------7

SOME PERSONAL QUESTIONS. PICK OUT YOURS.

(From Dr. Charles Sheldon's Church Calendar.)

1. Are you spending as much money for religion as for amusement?
2. Have you read your Bible this morning as much as the newspapers?
3. Do you have family worship or something to correspond to it?
4. Would your wife be surprised if you should kiss her when you leave the house to-morrow, or are you getting too old or too sanitary to kiss your wife? .Two questions.)
5. Did the last book you read have anything in it worth telling anybody?
6. Would you be willing to tell everybody here this morning where you were last night?
7. If you belong to the church, are you doing all you can for it as you promised you would when you joined it?
8. How long is it since you tried to get any one to be a Christian?
9. Would you be willing to tell this congregation how much money you made last week, and what you are going to do with it?
10. When was the last time you said a prayer in public or in private? Or don't you believe in prayer?
11. Are people always glad to meet you because you are so cheerful and helpful?
12. Who is the first person to whom you would go if you had Committed a great sin?
13. Do you have any friends to whom you feel perfectly free to go for a loan of money?
14. Are you perfectly certain where you are going when you die?

Upon the resignation of Dr. Hall, Mr. J. E. Wilkinson was elected president of the Mens Adult Federation of Bible Classes.

We urge all members to support the President and Executive Committee with some real work. The Executive Committee meets the second Sunday afternoon in every month at the Y. M. C. A. 3 oclock. We have great things ahead in Sunday School work if we co-operate, and this federation is the best means to that end.

EVERY SUNDAY MORNING

9:30

YOU WILL FIND OUR DOORS WIDE OPEN, AND A WARM
WELCOME.   COME THOU WITH US AND WE WILL DO
THEE GOOD.

FIRST CHRISTIAN CHURCH SUNDAY SCHOOL.

E. E. APPERSON, Supt.

SUNDAY MAY 27, 1917.

Bible School_____ _____ _____ 9:30

Lords Supper and Preaching _____11:00
    Penticost.

Endeavor _____ 7:00
    Financing the Kingdom, Luke 19; 11-26.

Evening Service _____ 8:00
    Types and Anti-Types.

Prayer Meeting Thursday Evening_____ _____7:30
    Saul; Shirking responsibility. 1 Sam. 9; 18-21.

7--------------------------------7

Have you subscribed for "Something Doing" better do it now.

7--------------------------------7

THE MAN ON HIS JOB.

I haven't much faith in the man who complains
  Of the work he has chosen to do.
He's lazy or else he's deficient in brains,
  And maybe a hypocrite too.
He's likely to cheat and he's likely to rob;
Away with the man who finds fault with his job!
But give me the man with the sun in his face,
  And the shadows all dancing behind;
Who meets his reverses with calmness and grace,
  And never forgets to be kind;
For whether he's wielding a scepter or swab,
I have faith in the man who's in love with his job.

7--------------------------------7

The Banker has to save in exactly the same way as the janitor who sweeps out the bank. B. S.

7--------------------------------7

There are still a few empty chairs in No. 7's Class Room.

PSYCHIST WRITES MERSEREAU PLAY

1,200 MILES FROM BROADWAY,
HE SENDS STAR JUST WHAT SHE ASKED

This Is a Universal "Story"

Much has been heard about messages being conveyed by spirits from the other world to hypnotists, phychists, psychoanalysts and all the other ists, but all of them were outdone, outclassed and outwitted the other evening when the Universal Film Manufacturing Company introduced to the world the first and only psychoscenarioist. His name is Edgar Cayce and he sent a psycho-scenario, four hundred and fifty words long, from Selma, Alabama, twelve hundred and eighty miles away, to room 1, in Churchill's, where Violet Mersereau, the dainty little Bluebird star, was sitting nervously surrounded by thirty newspaper men and trade journal representatives, awaiting the plot.

If the Universal accept this scenario, it will be the first written by a psycho-scenario writer, for not since the beginning of filmdom has a penner of plots attempted to do what Mr. Cayce did last Thursday evening.

It all started something like this: On December 13 last President Carl Laemmle received a mysterious letter from one Edwin Williamson, who in addition to acting as freight agent for the Southern Railway at Selma, fills in his spare time by acting as spiritual advisor, or spiritual business manager of Mr. Cayce. Just imagine what could be done if he could persuade his employer to apply the mental stuff to the transportation of all freight for the Southern Railway. Or, for example, imagine what the British Government would give to employ Cayce to go into these hypnotic sleeps and direct the course of their ships and German submarines!

In this letter Williamson said that he had a personal friend who was possessed of "an unusual gift, power or whatever it might be called." This friend was in the habit of going into a hypnotic sleep, from self-suggestion or otherwise, and then he conversed with the party who he went to sleep to. Mr. Williamson stated that he baffled physicians and has located lost articles and performed many other wonderful feats.

"If you are interested, and will write me, naming a date and the hour, allowing for the difference in time, which is one hour, stating the name of the party who you have in mind to take the lead in a photo-play, and tell me the street and house number where the party will be, I think I can surprise you."

Mr. Laemmle was so much impressed with the possibilities that he turned over the correspondence to the publicity department and instructed that the fellow be given an opportunity of showing what he could do.

Accordingly, it was decided to hold the test at Churchill's, and that Violet Mersereau, with a staff of newspaper men and trade journalists, be on hand to await the results.

The ceremonies were in charge of Nat Rothstein, advertising manager of the Universal, who explained to the gathering what it was all about, aided by speeches on psychology, etc., by Paul Gulick, Eustace Hale Ball, who is the author of the Universal's forthcoming serial, "The Voice on the Wire," and Dr. William E. Young, who is an authority on the subject of hypnotism, mental telepathy, self-suggestion and psychoanalysis.

A table was placed in the center of the room and on it was laid a piece of paper describing the sort of play Violet Mersereau would like for her next vehicle. This was at exactly 8.30, and the paper remained there for fifty minutes—the time required for the test. And all the time it was there Edgar Cayce was suggesting himself to sleep down there in tropical Selma.

During the interval the spirits were greatly aiding the committee, so that by the time the scenario arrived they were in an excellent frame of mind to receive the results of the test. Peter Milne of the Motion Picture News; Benny Grimm, Moving Picture World; Frederick Schrader, Variety; Arthur Ungar, New York Clipper; Ben Davis, New York Tribune, amused themselves while waiting for the psycho-scenario by singing a symphony, written by Joe Burrowes, on the spur of the moment, to Violet Mersereau, and which ran something like this:

Dear Violet Mersereau,
You've won our hearts, you know—
Star of the Universal,
A picture queen without rehearsal;
With your very charming face,
Your wondrous smile and grace,
You've won a nation's hearts
With your many leading parts.
Dear Violet Mersereau,
You're getting all the "dough."

At 2.35 Friday morning the psycho-scenario arrived. It proved to be just the sort of a play that Violet asked for previous to the beginning of the test. Mr. Cayce calls it "Through the Sublimal," and it is a five reeler. Miss Mersereau says she has turned it over to the scenario editor with the recommendation that it be prepared for her so that she can start on it as her next picture.

CHILD BURNED BY POWDER FLASH

Little Hugh Lynn Cayce, son of Mr. and Mrs. Edgar Cayce, was the victim of a bad accident at the studio of Mr. Cayce on Broad street yesterday.

The bright little fellow was in the studio and among some photographic supplies he came across a package of flashlight powder and was playing with it. Afterwards the little fellow struck a match and the head flew off into the powder, causing a quick and dangerous flash of fire, and the flames covered his face and head.

A physician was quickly secured and gave the injured child attention. He stated to Mr. and Mrs. Cayce that one of the eyes would certainly be saved and hopes that the other will also be saved, but cannot say as to the final outcome of the other eye.

Information this afternoon was to the effect that the little fellow was resting well and that hopes are held out for a speedy recovery. Mr. and Mrs. Cayce have many friends in Selma who deeply sympathise with them in this distressing accident.

There isn't a more appropriate photograph to accompany this newspaper article, from a 1914 issue of the Selma (Alabama) *Times-Journal,* on one of the classic examples of the Edgar Cayce readings healing cases (*There Is a River* devotes five pages to this incident, in Chapter 13). This particular picture was a commercial assignment for Edgar Cayce.

Another winning combination for the Cayce Art Company. However, I suspect that Gertrude might have had a smile on her pretty face in the photograph bought by the cotton merchant, which means that this is one of the perhaps half-dozen exposures Edgar made before he got one he was happy with. By the way, Gertrude used to help Edgar with some of his assignments, especially portraiture, to which she added oil colors and tinting, even doing some retouching.

(Left)   Mounted outside the studio door, once a day this clock would stop with a pointer on someone's picture, which was attached to the edge of that barely distinguishable disk. That person, as advertised, got his photo-finishing work free.

73

CAYCE STORY

IS SENSATION

IN THIS CITY

Feat of Speaking Through Telepathy or Spirit Medium or Other Means to New York a Marvel.

When The Journal was out Wednesday afternoon, carrying the story of The New York Morning Telegraph concerning Edgar Cayce and Edwin Williamson, two well known Selmians, it almost created a sensation in Selma.

The Selma Stationery's supply of New York papers having the Cayce story was soon gobbled up. In fact,

As a result of psychic readings that helped neighbors and his young brother, David E. Kahn became a devoted lifelong friend of the Cayces, and received many readings himself. (Below) Edgar stands behind two dear friends before they shipped overseas to fight in World War I. That's Lieutenant David E. Kahn, lower right, next to Major Alf Wilson (for details, see *My Life with Edgar Cayce*, as told to Will Oursler by David E. Kahn).

In December 1918 I received a request from a Mr. Thrash [GD's note: No copy on file] (*editor of a newspaper in Cleburne, Texas*) *for a Physical reading, also some questions as regarding business. Some letters passed before any information was given. Among these letters was one in which he asked for my birthdate, saying he desired to have my horoscope cast. Soon after this I received several communications from astrologers telling me that on March 19, 1919, I would be able to give a reading that would be of the most interest to mankind as a whole, than any I would be able to give during that year. I was asked to make this reading public. I did not care for notoriety (which I felt this would give), yet being curious and desiring to know what the reading would give at this time, I attempted it—and the following reading is the result. The questions asked in this reading were prepared by myself. The suggestion given at the time was something like this:*

[EC; ? Conductor; ? Steno. Selma, Ala.]
You will have before you the body and the enquiring mind of Edgar Cayce, and you will tell us how the psychic work is accomplished through this body, and will answer any other questions that I will ask you respecting this work.

Mr. C: *We have the body here—we have had it before. In this state the conscious mind is under subjugation of the subconscious or soul mind. The information obtained and given by this body is obtained through the power of mind over mind, or power of mind over physical matter, or obtained by the suggestion as given to the active part of the subconscious mind. It obtains its information from that which it has gathered, either from other subconscious minds—put in touch with the power of the suggestion of the mind controlling the speaking faculties of this body, or from minds that have passed into the Beyond, which leave their impressions and are brought in touch by the power of the suggestion. What is known to one subconscious mind or soul is known to another, whether conscious of the fact or not. The subjugation of the conscious mind putting the subconscious in action in this manner or in one of the other of the manners as described, this body obtains its information when in the subconscious state.*

Q-1. Is this information always correct?

A-1. Correct in so far as the suggestion is in the proper channel or in accord with the action of subconscious or soul matter.

Q-2. Do the planets have anything to do with the ruling of the destiny of men? If so, what? and what do they have to do with this body?

A-2. They do. In the beginning, as our own planet, Earth, was set in motion, the placing of other planets began the ruling of the destiny of all matter as created, just as the division of waters was and is ruled by the moon in its path about the Earth; just so as in the higher creation, as it began, is ruled by the action of the planets about the Earth.

The strongest power in the destiny of man is the Sun, first; then the closer planets, or those that are coming in ascendency at the time of the birth of the individual; but let it be understood here, no action of any planet or any of the phases of the Sun, Moon, or any of the heavenly bodies surpass the rule of man's individual will power—the power given by the Creator of man in the beginning, when he became a living soul, with the power of choosing for himself.

The inclination of man is ruled by the planets under which he is born. In given position of the solar system at the time of the birth of an individual, it can be worked out—that is, the inclinations and actions without the will power taken into consideration.

As in this body here [Edgar Cayce] born March 18, 1877, three minutes past three o'clock, with the Sun descending, on the wane, the Moon in the opposite side of the Earth (old moon), Uranus at its zenith, hence the body is ultra in its actions. Neptune closest in conjunction, or Neptune as it is termed in astrological survey, in the ninth house; Jupiter, the higher force of all the planets, save the Sun, in descendency, Venus just coming to horizon, Mars just set, Saturn —to whom all insufficient matter is cast at its decay—opposite the face of the Moon. Hence the inclination as the body is controlled by the astrological survey at the time of the birth of this body, either (no middle ground for this body) very good or very bad, very religious or very wicked, very rich or always losing, very much in love or hate, very much given to good works or always doing wrong, governed entirely by the will of the body. Will is the educational factor of the body; thence the patience, the persistence, the ever faithful attention that should be given to the child when it is young. [GD's note: I believe above birth data was volunteered because Mr. Thrash did not accept birth data from EC and parents.]

As to the forces of this body, the psychical is obtained through the action of Uranus and of Neptune, always it has been to this body and always will, just outside the action of firearms, yet ever within them, just saved financially and spiritually by the action of great amount of water—the body should live close to the sea, should always have done so. The body is strange to other bodies in all of its actions, in the psychical life, in all of its ideas as expressed in the spiritual life as to its position on all matters pertaining to political, religious or economical positions. This body will either be very rich or very poor.

Q-3. Will this work hurt the body?

A-3. Only through the action or power of suggestion over the body. This body is controlled in its work through the psychical or the mystic or spiritual. It is governed by the life that is led by the person who is guiding the subconscious when in this state, or by the line of thought that is given to create ideas of expression to the subconscious.

As the ideas given the subconscious to obtain its information are good, the body becomes better; if bad or wicked it becomes under the same control. Then the body should not be held responsible save through the body controlling the body at such times.

Q-4. Can this power be used to be of assistance to humanity and also to obtain financial gain?

A-4. There are many channels through which information obtained from this body in this state would be of assistance to humanity. To obtain financial gain from these is to obtain that which is just and right to those dependent upon this body for the things of life. Not those that would be destructive to the bodies themselves, physically or mentally, but that which is theirs by right should be obtained for such information.

As to which is the best channel, it depends as to whether the information desired is in accord with the ideas of the body from which they are attempting to obtain them.

When credence is given to the work in a material way, anyone is willing to pay in a financial way for such information; but without credence there can be nothing obtained.

A-5.   *The body should keep close in touch with the spiritual side of life; with sincerity to the spiritual side of life, if he is to be successful, mentally, physically, psychically and financially.*

The safest brace is the spiritual nature of the body; sincerity of the work done or obtained through any channel with which this body is connected is governed by the masses through the action of the body towards the spiritual.

[*5/24/23 See 257-1 answering questions about EC and Penn-Tenn Fuel Corp. 10/8/23 See first of 3744 series in re astrology and EC's psychic data. 2/9/24 See EC's first Life Reading, 294-8.*]

9/16/35 EC's ltr. to ⚸516: ". . . I was born on March 18, 1877, in Hopkinsville, Christian County, Kentucky, at 1:30 o'clock on a Sunday afternoon. However, I have had several astrologers tell me it was impossible for me to have been born at that time, else I would have been a girl. But this is the actual record from my parents, the physician, and the birth certificate record . . ." [See GD's notation under 294-8 report.]

3/19/40 See EC's letter in re 254-2 under 951-4 report.

Whether or not this was a self-portrait is beside the point. It just happens to be an excellent dual portraiture and my favorite of any the Cayces made or had taken. Both seem so perky and full of vitality that it inspires one . . . do you feel it? In Selma, about 1917.

This certainly appears to be a proud father looking more as if it is his first son than his third (the Cayces' second child died as an infant). This is Edgar Evans Cayce, born February 9, 1918, who later chose his own nickname—"Ecken"— through enunciation difficulties. That's not the most relaxed way to hold a baby you'll ever see, but it certainly shows lots of love. Edgar Cayce possessed a natural rapport with children all of his life.

"Ecken" with an affectionate girl friend, Anne Elizabeth Gray, who (at right) plants a kiss on his nose. One wonders if this might not have been a parental suggestion, possibly from the proud photographer father.

(Left) These menfolk in Gertrude's life were quite possibly photographed by her, after Edgar made the initial set up with camera and lights. Even if it was self-tripped, it's a well-composed photo and has character, though a bit solemn, which might have been the way she wanted it. The Cayces mailed this out on postcards. (Below) Edgar Cayce with his Junior Christian Endeavor champions at the 1920 state convention held in Birmingham. That is Hugh Lynn kneeling, second from the left in the front row. Undoubtedly, Gertrude is again tripping the camera, which may have something to do with Edgar's concerned look, or it may relate to oil well drilling difficulties constantly beleaguring their Texas venture near San Saba. (The oil wells were a means of raising money for building a hospital, an idea David E. Kahn got when he returned from the war. The Cayce psychic readings told them the hospital should be built at Virginia Beach, then a small fishing village east of Norfolk, Virginia). Here, even Hugh Lynn seems detached.

A Hospital Proposed By the Friends and Invalids Who Have Been Benefited or Cured By Edgar Cayce

MR. EDGAR CAYCE
whose ambition to establish a sanitarium or hospital in the South where his rare powers of healing can be dispensed to suffering humanity.

Since October 4, 1922, Edgar Cayce, the healer and mystic man of this day, has been located at the Tutwiler Hotel, Room 1006, Birmingham, Alabama. During the period Mr. Cayce has been here he has given readings for more than one hundred and fifty men, women and children, giving them in many cases a treatment outlined by him, as he calls it when asleep, but there is one condition that he desires well founded, that either the patient or some friend close to the patient make the request for the reading, then he will very cheerfully do the work. And, when he wakes up he does not know a word that he has said or a suggestion that he has made for the cure or relief of the body that was before him, and for this reason it is necessary for someone to be present, who can write the reading (he has a stenographer to do this) as it is given in order that the patient can have a copy of the reading, so as to follow the instructions as given. A very peculiar thing about it all is that the patient does not need to be present when the reading is given. However, Mr. Cayce would very much prefer to have them present or at least some of the patient's very close friends. The reason is simply this, when they hear the diagnosis spoken by the man who is asleep and describes their condition so very minutely it only then gives them the absolute confidence, and they then will follow the treatment suggested. However, sometimes the treatment is very simple even when operations have been advised by others. When the treatment is carried out to the letter in accordance with Mr. Cayce's suggestions there is not known a case in twenty years that the results promised by him when he is in this sleep or subconscious condition but what has been just as he prescribed, either materially benefited or cured. Occasionally there are individuals who come before him that he says are beyond repair, meaning that they cannot be cured, but a very low per cent and the writer believes that two per cent would cover the cases that has come under his notice that are "beyond repair," as he expresses it when in the subconscious state. To any that this notice comes before can call at the hotel designated to see Mr. Cayce and consult with him. There is no charge for that and neither is there a specific charge made for diagnosis of any individual. However, most all of the patients very cheerfully donate a reasonable fee to help take care of the expenses incurred by him for doing this work. He will yet remain at the above address for at least two weeks, when at that time he will probably fill an engagement at Miami, Fla., where many people are anxious to have his services.

Newspaper coverage of Edgar Cayce's activities and prospects of a hospital, wherein his psychic readings could be put to work, was quite extensive in Birmingham, Alabama, during 1922. (*Birmingham Age-Herald*)

Next page: the original photograph for the above article.

81

THE BIRMINGHAM AGE-HERALD
October 1922

PSYCHOLOGY STUDY CLUB AND GUESTS HEAR MR. CAYCE.

The Psychology Study Club, composed of 20 women who are giving serious consideration to matters of mental science, makes it a point to invite worth-while speakers to appear before their number, and with this end in view, they called together 50 representative women of the city as their guests on Tuesday morning, when Mr. Edgar Cayce, the psychic diagnostician, was the principal speaker. This club is exclusive in membership, but liberal in views.

"Who would have imagined 25 years ago," said Mr. Cayce, "that a company of 50 refined, cultured women in a city of this size would have acknowledged an interest in, much less have gathered together to listen to one who really practices psychical healing?"

Mrs. J. D. Head, a member of the club, thus speaks of the gathering.

The speaker then proceeded, in his simple, earnest way to tell of his first efforts toward being of service to his fellow man. He told how he discovered that he had the ability to lose himself in sleep and find himself in the presence of a great healing power, and how he is able, while in that state, to answer questions concerning the ills of body and mind of his patients. He described the impressions received from the healing power which appears to him as a great light.

Mr. Cayce freely answered all the questions which were propounded by those who were privileged to hear him. These questions related to spirit communion, reincarnation, prevision on public questions, and the acquirement of psychic power. Mr. Cayce is absolutely loyal when it comes to discussing matters where confidence has been reposed in him. Where readings have been given concerning national or world affairs they have been made a matter of record, and future generations will become aware of them.

An affecting moment occurred when one of his patients who was present told in a voice choked with emotion of having received his sight by following the advice of Mr. Cayce.

None of the cures is recounted in a boastful way, the speaker does not claim any glory for himself, but there is one that must be told because it struck the assembly as being the most remarkable of all. This was the case of a defective child in New York City, whose parents were able, by following the suggestion of Mr. Cayce, to bring the child to a normal condition, after it had been an idiot for six years. The amount of medicine given in this particular case was negligible.

Mr. Cayce was asked by one of the prominent women at the meeting to recount his interviews with Dr. Munsterburg and with Sir Oliver Lodge.

"Dr. Munsterburg," said the speaker, "came blustering into Hopkinsville, Ky., where I then resided, without any previous warning. 'Cayce,' he said, 'I've come to expose you. I've shown up many a fraud. Where is your cabinet.'"

"'I haven't got any, sir.'"

"'Then where is your seance room?'"

"'I don't have any, sir.'"

"'Well, where are some of your patients?' bellowed the doctor. He was cited to numbers of the rank and file among the citizens of the town. The doctor left, only to return the next morning in a different frame of mind.

"'Cayce,' he said, 'I have seen them and talked with them, and if you had cured only one it would be the most remarkable thing in the world. Even if it is all a guess, I must say you are the darnedest best guesser I have ever heard of.'"

Sir Oliver Lodge's opinion of Mr. Cayce is characteristic, in that he believes that when the latter enters into the sleep state, the spirit of some departed physician takes possession of the body and talks with Mr. Cayce's voice. Mr. Cayce does not believe in spiritualism in the ordinary acceptation of the word, but he does not argue these questions, allowing every one to air his own opinion.

With one accord the guests of the Psychology Study Club voiced impressions of the speaker in one word—sincerity.

BIRMINGHAM AGE-HERALD
October 1922

POWER CREDITED
TO GOD

"Healer" Says His Work Is Done Through Divine Gift.

"Whatever powers in healing I may possess I attribute to God working through me for the welfare of the afflicted," declared Edgar Cayce in an informal address to the Psychology Club Tuesday night at the courthouse. "I regard the religious phase, and not the psychic, the most important part of the work. To me the challenge continues that I must practice discrimination in the cases I treat, and that whatever is done must be done for His sake; that whatever feeble powers I possess must be dedicated to Him."

A substantial audience greeted the Selma mystic in Judge Smith's courtroom at 8 o'clock and many questions were asked the speaker concerning his healing work. Since his return to Birmingham after almost a year's absence, Mr. Cayce has been in constant demand for his "readings," which are declared to be remarkable by his friends and those who claim to have been cured by his diagnosis and advice.

While in Birmingham, Mr. Cayce will be at the Tutwiler Hotel. After he feels that he must pass on to other cities to assist, if he can, those who have called upon him for relief, he will resume his work in other fields. Meanwhile, his purpose holds to build a great sanatorium for healing the afflicted, those for whom the physicians have done all they could —a great hospital somewhere where he may do in a much broader and bigger way what he must perforce now be doing on a small scale. Several cities have offered to endow such a hospital for him but his plans as yet are not perfectly crystallized.

BIRMINGHAM AGE-HERALD
October 1922

Edgar Cayce To Speak To Local Theosophists

The Birmingham Theosophical Society invites the public to attend a lecture on Friday evening, November 3, at 8 o'clock at headquarters, fifth floor, Cable Hall Building, when Edgar Cayce, psychic and mystic, will address the society and its friends.

Throughout the world today thousands of thoughtful human beings are finding solace and intellectual pleasure in theosophy in its broad and liberal conceptions of man and his place on this planet. It is a sort of pan-religion that finds good in all religions and teaches the brotherhood of mankind and welcomes any discussion or investigation that seeks as its objective more truth and light for the human race.

Mr. Cayce's address will deal largely with his work in healing, and those interested in the amelioration of disease and suffering through faith and belief in higher powers are cordially invited to attend. During the last year the headquarters have been made attractive, and the society at all times welcomes the people to open meetings of the lodge.

BIRMINGHAM AGE-HERALD
October 1922

A Hospital of Last Resort Proposed By Invalids Served By Edgar Cayce

For thirty days or more Edgar Cayce, healer and mystic, has been besieged by invalids seeking a cure for diseases that have been given up by the physicians. During the period, Mr. Cayce has given "readings" for approximately a hundred men, women and children, giving light and direction and new hope to many who had been led to believe that there was no hope for them. Patiently, but assiduously, this gentle, kind-hearted man is doing all that he can to relieve distress locally. Constantly, throughout the day at his headquarters at the Tutwiler Hotel, he is being appealed to for aid. Three times daily for a month he has appealed to that hidden sanctuary for diagnosis and for treatment of the diseases that come before him, and there is no record of failure. Whatever be the spiritual nature of the source on which he draws, Mr. Cayce is convinced, through thousands of cases of cures obtained through his "readings," that he is but a humble instrument of God.

Through his success with local invalids, friends of Mr. Cayce have convinced him that Birmingham is the logical site for the establishment of that hospital and sanatorium for which he has planned and dreamed for more than twenty years. Citizens of Denver, Colo., of Columbus, O., and other cities that have entertained the healer and have been benefited by his service have besought him to locate elsewhere. But being Southern-born, and loving the South, he has decided that if Birmingham wants the hospital he will stay here. And, in explanation of that statement, it should be said here that Mr. Cayce has nothing to sell: that he has never commercialized his remarkable powers and never proposes to do so. Himself a man of simple life, "contented with small means, seeking refinement rather than fashion," seeking above all to serve the wretched ones of earth, and desiring above all else to have a hospital where all who need his services may come, certainly there should be a sufficient number of persons here to back him financially in this beautiful venture he proposes. One thing is definitely sure: That unless his clients who have been comforted and healed and unless the public at large give that support in this emergency, some other hospital somewhere will be occupied by him.

BIRMINGHAM AGE-HERALD
October 1922

"PECULIAR GIFT HAS BEEN MINE SINCE YOUTH," SAYS MR. CAYCE

MYSTICISM, PSYCHISM, OR
WHAT YOU WILL,
ENVELOPS MAN WHOSE POWER IN
HEALING HAS
CREATED TREMENDOUS INTEREST AMONG
ALL CONDITIONS OF MEN

By Dolly Dalrymple

"During the twenty-two years in which I have given whatever gifts I possess for the benefit of suffering humanity, I have diagnosed eight thousand and fifty-six cases and prescribed cures for them, all of whom I have been told were satisfactory."

The statement by Mr. Edgar Cayce, native Kentuckian and for many years a resident of Alabama, was as unboastfully made as possible, when he was talking to me yesterday.

Quiet in his demeanor, modest in his speech, with none of the flare and glare of the "professional" mystic, psychic, clairvoyant, or fortune teller, Mr. Cayce, who now makes his home in Selma, is a visitor to Birmingham for a few days, having come here to meet a group of people from Chicago who desired his service.

"How do I do it?" Mr. Cayce repeated the question after me. "I can't any more tell than you can; one thing I know and that is since I was a child I have had the peculiar gift; my parents used to thrash me soundly for my ideas and practice of my powers, and yet that did not deter me from going straight ahead and revealing them to all with whom I came in contact."

Testimonials

From Maine to California, from Florida to Canada, Mr. Cayce has letters, all of which he has preserved most carefully in a valuable book from some of the most prominent physicians and scientists of this age, among them Dr. McDougal of Harvard, before whom Mr. Cayce appeared in person and revealed his gift.

Dr. Munsterberg also granted Mr. Cayce an audience, declaring that he expected to expose him to the world.

Mr. Cayce repeats the incident as follows:

"Dr. Munsterberg accosted me with the questions:

"Where are your patients? Can you call them in?

"Certainly I said and did so, after which Dr. Munsterberg declared that he could not call my work a fake, for my patients were there to testify to my ability."

Christianity the Foundation

"My work is not for pecuniary purposes; my patients pay me what they will. By profession I am a photographer. I have never been on the stage although I have had the most flattering offers. In fact I refused fifteen thousand dollars to appear for three times on the stage and demonstrate my work in a nearby city, a short time ago, but I shun such publicity and notoriety."

"Then how do you do it if it is not like the professional psychic medium or clairvoyant?"

"In the privacy of my own rooms," said Mr. Cayce. "Yes, I go into a trance or sub-conscious state; what it is I don't know; I am really not aware that I am doing any thing marvelous; in fact I am not conscious of what I am saying or prescribing; I just don't know what it is."

"This I do know; that it is man's humanity to man to be able to diagnose suffering and disease and prescribe a remedy for it that cures!"

" 'May the words of my mouth and the meditations of my heart be acceptable in Thy sight, O Lord, my strength and my redeemer,' is the foundation of my work. Belief in the fatherhood of God and the brotherhood of man is my motto and for this reason I hope to be able to establish a hospital or a sanitarium so that suffering humanity can have the benefit of my gifts."

Not Spiritualism, But Spirituality

"No; I do not believe in spiritualism but I do believe in spirituality," declared Mr. Cayce. "What those who say they communicate with the dead must mean is, that they communicate with impressions left by the dead here. They talk to the personality of the dead; in other words the personality which is left to us here just as the individuality goes into the other world.

"Ectoplasm, of which we hear so much, is nothing more or less than personality reduced to this form. Thoughts are deeds we are told and they may become miracles or they may become crimes.

"Japan once proposed a law preventing people from thinking wrong, if you recall; in other words, right thinking on any subject prevents crime and reduces suffering to a marked degree."

"The professional mystic, mind reader, who blindfolded on the stage tells you the number of your watch, the color of your sweetheart's hair, who your next husband will be, what of him," I asked curiously.

"I couldn't call any such people fakes, because I don't know what they are or what they see or what they feel, any more than I could call myself a fake because I don't know where my power comes from or whither it goes."

A Physical Phenomenon

Mr. Cayce is very baffling, very unusual and very interesting, certainly one of those physical phenomenals, which puzzle and confound the layman, while exerting equally an unrestful effect upon the scientific mind.

One thing I will say for the peculiarly gifted Mr. Cayce.

I don't believe the hundreds of people whose written testimonials (he has many of them in their own hand writing) would put down on cold white paper such startling statements regarding his powers, if he had not benefited them in some measure.

At any rate Mr. Cayce's case is interesting, whether psychic, mystic, clairvoyant, mind reader or spiritualist, what you will. It is not for me to say or you and he has the foundation of successful achievement written luminously upon his life work in the simple fact that he believes in himself!

Anne Elizabeth Gray, a Model T Ford, and Edgar Evans Cayce pose for a snapshot taken by Mrs. Gray (that might be Gertrude Cayce in the car behind the wheel . . . Edgar was undoubtedly out in the wilds of oil well country). No, you haven't tilted the book, the snapshot was taken slightly out of whack. This was Edgar Evans' kiss-on-the-nose girl friend from a previous page . . . hardly seems like the same girl, right?

Still the closest of buddies since childhood, Hugh Lynn Cayce poses with Thomas Burr House, Jr. (Tommy), during Hugh Lynn's infrequent visits at "the hill" (Hopkinsville), where someone of the family played photographer in Edgar Cayce's absence. This possibly was just prior to Hugh Lynn's trip to Texas, also, to find out for the family what was going on at the oil diggings. He did much of the picture-taking honors at the two scenes below. First is the main street of San Saba, then Edgar Cayce and Dr. House cleaning up after dining on fresh fish they had caught earlier from that body of water (presumably a lake) visible beyond them. Hugh Lynn also took the car scene on page 92.

The motley group above just happens to be Edgar Cayce (being leaned against left of center) and his oil well drilling associates, more than likely near San Saba. In his own handwriting, Edgar had written each man's name either directly below or above him, and I assure you that they aren't any more legible on the original photograph than they are here. (At right) At the site of the oil digs, probably in 1922, Edgar posed some 100 meters uphill from the drilling tower. Notice the figure of a man behind and beyond him (for size and distance comparison) next to sloped shed, or two black and two white horses about 800 meters (half mile) above and beyond the same shed.

With Edgar Cayce and David Kahn off tending the oil well drilling, the Squire fell heir to photographic duty, which he had done before on special occasions. Little did he know, nor could he have guessed, when he photographed these two lovely young cousins, Gladys and Mildred Davis, that one of them would become Edgar's stenographer in another year (Gladys at left). It was through the influence of Arthur Lammers, with the Squire's help, that Gertrude and Edgar were convinced of the need for a competent stenographer to record the readings, a decision that delighted Gertrude.

(Above right) Edgar poses with his fishing buddy, G. K. Nicodemus, who (right) stands in his fishing boat in a rather unusual pose, maybe just to show his catch and his outfit. He also had served as conductor in some of the readings.

It was my original intent to include two or three Cayce verbatim readings here for your perusal, or pertinent extracts. But, after researching them, I learned there is no one reading that spells out the whole situation, none expressing the growing problems, nor one that simplified the recommended operating procedures—which were never followed *fully* at any time. Therein lies the camel's back-breaking straw.

In order to include verbatim extracts of pertinent readings that would clarify the situation to a mutual understanding, you would have had to struggle through no less than eight pages. You have already read the strange idiosyncratic ramblings of other Cayce psychic readings ("clairvoyant" was used then as a less dirty word in that time period, used well into the '60s before "psychic" became acceptable), and more are included throughout the book. Without a familiarity with this material, one can easily get lost in the words, many of which seem to relate back into Bible eras.

Most of the Cayce oil well readings (cross-indexed under a common heading, land:, possibly because such items as minerals relate to this area), of which there are hundreds, are under a few individual numbers, including one for the Cayce Petroleum Company (3,777)—a legally registered enterprise that accumulated oil well drilling land leases (mineral rights) in at least four states (Arkansas, Oklahoma, Texas, and Florida). However, there is no evidence that Edgar Cayce, the Cayce Petroleum Co., or the later Association of National Investigators (A.R.E.'s predecessor) ever realized taxable funds from any of the successful drillings made by other companies in later years (after the Cayce leases expired), despite the many readings given toward development of potential financial security, or construction of hospital facilities.

Not only did Edgar Cayce continue giving readings for oil well "wildcatters" after moving to Dayton, Ohio, then to Virginia Beach, but some of those entities involved in oil well readings into the late '30s are still active in A.R.E. operations today.

These particular readings emphasized there was a lack of complete trust among drilling operation associates, that suspicion and jealousy altered attitudes, ideals and purposes, they would not have attracted the vandalism directed by competing oil drillers, which eventually put them out of business through subversive destruction of property, expired land leases, and lack of financial backing. Unfair as it may seem, where the readings were used for selfish interests no good came of that effort and Edgar Cayce generally suffered from it in the end (more than just a headache, too). While the earliest oil well readings are missing, there is correspondence in the files that verifies their existence. After Gladys Davis set up a filing system in 1923, very few readings got lost, except, perhaps, where Edgar Cayce entrusted them to particular investigators (there are probably other readings, several on buried treasure and on Atlantis are missing, as an example . . . undoubtedly occurring before the master file system and microfilming took place, where researchers worked directly with the original).

Rather than devote more words and space to explaining the oil well drilling predicament Cayce involved himself in, I would suggest that the reader obtain a copy of *The Outer Limits of Edgar Cayce's Power,* by Edgar Evans Cayce and Hugh Lynn Cayce, wherein two chapters are devoted to this very subject.

A Cayce family portrait taken by the Squire in 1922.

(Below) David E. Kahn's new Marmon touring sedan being held on the ground by Edgar Cayce's foot on its running board (What's a running board? Ask your grandfather!) near San Saba, where all sorts of complications concerning the oil leases had set in. Vandalism by competing oil drillers finally drove them out of Texas. (Below) On a fishing expedition out of Miami, with influential friends, Edgar still hoped to gain financial support for the Birmingham hospital project.

With Edgar away so much, or preoccupied with giving readings, lecturing, and trying to locate financial support for the proposed hospital, the Squire took on the Cayce Art Studio chores, right up to important portraiture, including this lovely blond young lady, Gladys Davis (right), who had just been hired as Edgar's secretary, September 1923. While visiting and giving readings earlier in Dayton, Ohio, Edgar had met Arthur Lammers (no photo available), a wealthy printer, whose enthusiasm over possibilities of working with the readings, decided him on moving the Cayces to Dayton. Through Arthur Lammers' influence, many important changes came about in Edgar's life.

Edgar had gone ahead to Dayton with Arthur Lammers, where the readings produced such inspiring results in only a few days that it was decided to have Gertrude close the Selma studio and move Ecken and Miss Davis to Dayton (Hugh Lynn would stay and finish high school). Reincarnation was one of the invigorating subjects that raised eyebrows, including those of Linden Shroyer, Lammers' accountant, shown here with Gladys and Edgar. Shroyer was to become a great asset in this business of the readings, even when the Cayce family moved to Virginia Beach two years later.

It isn't difficult to determine who is doing snapshot assignments in this series of pictures, simply by taking note of who is present and who is not. It just happens that Edgar Cayce is missing from all three of these poses, but I doubt very much that it was a camera of his choosing, because of the overall fuzziness—an out-of-focus look—which was more than likely caused by an oily fingerprint on the lens (it's like shooting a picture through a dirty window). You'll have to agree that this Dayton city park makes a beautiful setting for a family outing, hosted by the Linden Shroyer family.

This lovely outing was possibly a farewell party just prior to the Cayces moving from Dayton, judging from the overall glum facial expressions. You ladies can get a good idea of the fashions again for this place and period from what these ladies are wearing. Gladys and Gertrude could not really afford anything elegant, but they did seem to dress well. You might enjoy Glady's own words about this very situation, found in *My Years with Edgar Cayce, The Personal Story of Gladys Davis Turner,* written by Mary Ellen Carter. You men might be interested in those bow ties.

(Above) More good comments were inspired by this back-yard charmer than by any other picture in the A.R.E. Headquarters exhibit; Gladys Davis and Gertrude Cayce sharing Ecken's wagon in the Cayce back yard (322 Grafton Avenue, Dayton, Ohio) this spring of '24. Arthur Lammers' business failed earlier, he withdrew financial support, and Linden Shroyer moved away to find another job. This restored Gertrude to the position of reading conductor. Through David Kahn, Morton Blumenthal obtained readings, which led to ideas of financing construction of a hospital again; and other readings directed them to leave this area, to settle in Virginia Beach. (Right) Perhaps W. L. Jones and Edgar Cayce were discussing those readings' strange implications.

On an overcast day, this Dayton outing for Gladys, Ecken, and Gertrude (upper right) was being shared with W. L. Jones, shown in lower right picture. All were taking notice of historical relics. Gladys was briefly separated from the Cayces after Thanksgiving when her father died, sending her home to comfort her mother and the four younger children (Tiny just seventeen, though married; Boyd, thirteen; Burt, eleven; Lucile only eight; while Gladys herself was at the ripe old age of nineteen).

(Below left) Young Edgar Evans sits astride his older brother's knee. Hugh Lynn's expression may be one of discomfort as the result of sitting in that wheelbarrow—not necessarily from squinting into the sun—or he may have been anxious to get back to work.

W. L. Jones again with Edgar, whose left hand is securely held in that of his young son, Ecken (right). Never one for wearing hats, except when modeling for his photographer father in his earlier years, here we find Hugh Lynn in a straw hat (below center left) and sporting his first eyeglasses. Jones looks the part of a cigar-smoking carnival barker.

(Right) Four scowling Cayces could reflect this family's frustrations in Dayton, especially when the readings suggested another move, this time to an unknown fishing village, just south of the mouth of Chesapeake Bay: Virginia Beach, Virginia. It had been less than two years since they left Selma, too.

98

Quite obviously this belongs with the earlier Dayton outing because it's identifiable right down to the same fuzziness found in those park scenes. It was probably camera-composed by Linden Shroyer. I include this for two reasons: it's an interesting study of Cayce faces, in or out of focus, and Hugh Lynn had always liked it . . . "great picture to show!"

Another picture somewhat out of chronology, this limited Cayce reunion in DeLand, Florida, has Edgar's second sister, Ola, looking the part of a fashion model, while her baby, held safely on the table by her husband, is hypnotized by the cameraman (or woman). Peering out of the noon shadow of his cap is Edgar Evans Cayce, also attracted to the camera. From the clasp of Edgar's hands atop the table, I can almost hear him telling them the news of hospital construction plans, and his tentative fund-raising meetings elsewhere in Florida.

99

This psychic reading given by Edgar Cayce at Phillips Hotel, Room 115, Dayton, Ohio, this 8th day of May, 1924, in accordance with request made by Mr. Edgar Cayce himself.

PRESENT

Edgar Cayce; Linden Shroyer, Conductor; Gladys Davis, Steno. George S. Klingensmith.

READING

Time of Reading	WORK	Phillips Hotel,
12:30 P.M.		*Dayton, Ohio*

Mr. S: *It has been given in a reading that when Mr. Cayce was ready to establish the Institute the forces would direct as to how this should be done. The forces have been asked before to give the best location for this Institute. Will they tell us now, under the present conditions and circumstances, where would be the best place to locate, and how to go about to establish such a place? What would be the first thing to do?*

Mr. C: *As has been given, the better place to establish such an Institute would be near large bodies of water, preferably on the East Coast at or near Virginia Beach, Va. As to how to establish such a place, as has been given, the work, the phenomena, the help, the assistance, the development, the force of development, the richness of the subject matter to be investigated through such an Institute, only needs be presented to such peoples as are, have been and may be interested in the development of mankind from this viewpoint, to obtain that necessary for the establishment of such an Institute. As to the first thing to be done, interest those first who have directly received direct or indirect benefits from work already performed. Do that.*

Be not faint-hearted, using discretion and retaining ever the principles of service to fellow man.

(GD's note: We have no record of earlier mentioning of Virginia Beach as a place for the work, though EC told us that the place was recommended in some of the earliest readings—of which no copies were kept.

EC told us that Gertrude's uncle and his wife, Mr. & Mrs. Hiram P. Salter, had gone on a vacation to Virginia Beach in 1915 and had reported that it was just a tiny fishing village; Mr. Salter could not understand why the readings insisted that the Edgar Cayce work should be established in or near Virginia Beach.)

VIRGINIA BEACH, Contemplated Move

This psychic reading given by Edgar Cayce at his office, 322 Grafton Avenue, Dayton, Ohio, this 30th day of June, 1925, in accordance with request made by [900].

PRESENT

Edgar Cayce; Mrs. Cayce, Conductor; Gladys Davis, Steno.
Mrs. Elizabeth E. Evans and Hugh Lynn Cayce.

READING

[254]

Time of Reading
3:00 P.M. Dayton Savings Time

Mrs. C: *You will have before you the work (psychic work) of Edgar Cayce, his contemplated move to Virginia Beach. You will also have in this connection the body and the mind of [900], of . . . Road, . . . N. J., and his connection with this work, also his business, his brother, and their families, all the conditions and circumstances surrounding same. Tell how the move to Virginia Beach may be facilitated, and if now, all the above regarding Edgar Cayce and [900] considered, is the right time, and answer the following questions.*

Mr. C: *Yes, we have the psychic work here of Edgar Cayce, and the conditions, mind, business associations, of [900], with his connection with same, and the contemplated move to Virginia Beach and those conditions as surround same.*

These conditions as present themselves, with the body and bodies as concerned with this, have been presented to the body, mind, of [900], and the circumstance that may be expected to arise from the action in regard to same has been given. The facilitation then of the circumstance and conditions must be judged by self, and through self's will acted upon, for with the condition as has been presented, it has been given that necessary for justification of self and self's attitude toward such.

As to the work and the psychic forces, as given, it has been set as from whence the beginning of such work should be begun (hasn't changed), for those elements that do give that motive, incentive, force, element, those urges, come through the association and surroundings from this place.

Ready for questions.

Q-1. Would it be best for [900] to accompany Edgar Cayce, to help in finding location?
A-1. Would, for in this the work, the elements of same, must show in each and every individual desiring the most from same, that element of interest in same. Same as is given in this: Those who would seek God must believe that He IS.

Q-2. In light of present conditions and people surrounding [900] in business and in home, how may [900] arrange this?
A-2. When the entity, body, mind, has been set at the purpose to do, then that necessary condition to accomplish same will be presented in a way and manner for same. For, under the existing conditions in and about the place where the elements of the work should be established, are not in that way of obtaining same at the present time, and will not be so until the seventh (7th) day of September.

101

This we find in North Virginia Beach, near the line of Plat 42, on the way from **254-23**
the North and South Beach, with the point of the line (trolley) in the rear.

Q-3. Would it be advisable for Edgar Cayce and [900] to make the trip at the present, to make arrangements for the move to Virginia Beach?

A-3. August 10th to 15th.

Q-4. Then, when should the move be made?

A-4. At once. When arrangements have been completed.

Q-5. Explain just what has been given, in reference to September 7th. What is the meaning of this date?

A-5. On that date, the place from which the start should be made will be obtainable. Not until then.

[Observation by GD, 6/2/48: September 7th, 1925, was Labor Day, the end of Virginia Beach's summer crowds, etc.]

Q-6. Should Edgar Cayce wait until that time to move the family?

A-6. Be there at that time, with all. Family, office and all!

Q-7. Any further suggestions or advice regarding these conditions and circumstances?

A-7. Only that as would be regarding that already given to the body, [900], in regards to same.

> *We are through.*

8/11/25 See reading ⚹900-108 re. visit and move to Virginia Beach.

WORK OF EDGAR CAYCE   **254-24**
VIRGINIA BEACH, Why?

This psychic reading given by Edgar Cayce at his office, 322 Grafton Avenue, Dayton, Ohio, this 15th day of August, 1925, in accordance with request made by Edgar Cayce himself.

PRESENT

Edgar Cayce; Mrs. Cayce, Conductor; Gladys Davis, Steno.
Mr. W. L. Jones and Hugh Lynn Cayce.

READING

[254]

Time of Reading   *322 Grafton Avenue,*
3:20 P.M. Dayton Savings Time

Mrs. C: *You will have before you Edgar Cayce, present in this room, and his family, and conditions surrounding same. Also [900] of . . . Road, . . . New Jersey, and conditions surrounding him, also the associations between Edgar Cayce and [900], also conditions in and around Virginia Beach, as related to the association of these two, [900] and Edgar Cayce, and their association with psychic phenomena. You will please give any information to any or all of these that will assist in making the success as has been given as regarding the move to Virginia Beach. You will please answer any questions I may ask you regarding any of these conditions.*

Mr. C: *Yes, many, many, suggestions may be given for the good of all* **254-24** *associated with the work; it needs the instruction and purpose necessary to make same succeed in the way and manner as has been given, for we find this has been approached from many angles. Then, to give that that would be beneficial, we would first begin from the locations and why.*

In the reasoning from the physical plane, the action of the environmental conditions we find creating a condition through which certain forces may manifest in an easy or a hard manner, see? For instance, easier for electricity to pass over iron than over glass, see?

Then, in the environmental forces in and about Virginia Beach and vicinity, there is that necessary for the reaching of many peoples of many climes, see? for the close proximity of the various spheres of active study in the various channels of education are through centers as will be found in touch with these channels, see? and from same a radiation would reach to a much broader field than has been possible heretofore.

Now with same there may be expected that condition that would bring some consternation through the channels of opposition. Yet this, as we find, is the place, the time and the action then necessary. For those vibrations of the universal forces, as manifest through the physical human body that relates to transmission of those elements of universal forces, bring the greater action on the body through which the phenomena will be manifested in or near this place—Virginia Beach, see?

The field, then, of activity is the broader, for there is the close proximity to the Capitol of the world, with sufficient distance to present the work in a more beneficial, beneficent, manner.

There is close proximity to the ports of the world and those reasonings as come with peoples of the sea.

These all go to make up that necessary.

Then, the individuals that are interested as given here: First the work of [900] is near to this place, and sufficient distance that the physical forces lend rather than retard in the development of same. Then the time of the development in the forces of [900] is in that place of being able to radiate sufficient to lend assistance in the way in which this would be most beneficial.

The manner and way would then be, for the work, from [900]'s viewpoint, to connect in such a manner the work with all phases of the developing as is manifested through the developing of the body.

As to those of the family, Edgar Cayce, these we find, all, will in many ways be improved, provided they take advantage of same, in the associations in this place, see?

Q-1. Which is more advisable, for Edgar Cayce to go direct to Virginia Beach or meet [900] in New York and then go to Virginia Beach?

A-1. Meet [900] in New York, then go to Virginia Beach.

Q-2. In regard to trip to Virginia Beach, in preparation for move there, should Edgar Cayce's son, Hugh Lynn Cayce, go to Virginia Beach to lend assistance in any way?

A-2. Very good—for as given, be well that all would go and lend assistance, for if the place does good to all, then all need to receive more good, see?

Q-3. Please give Edgar Cayce information necessary for him to know as to why Virginia Beach is the proper place for him to work from. Also outlining to him the line of procedure when he is located at or near Virginia Beach to make the work the success that readings have given can be made.

A-3. As to why has been given. As to the conduct of the body, physical, this has been given in many ways, for the one is the same as the other. First and foremost, as has been given, let this be the criterion for the endeavors: The work in all its phases is judged by the physical attendance to those things spiritual, and the aid in spiritual manners and social manners, as are given to those, for the reflection of each and every work is shown in the individual's relations to others.

Then give of self to others, calling on Him, the giver of all good and perfect gifts, to direct the way, and He is faithful to give to those who would seek Him in no uncertain way, see?

WORK OF EDGAR CAYCE
PROPHECY

This psychic reading given by Edgar Cayce at Southland Hotel, Norfolk, Virginia, this 20th day of August, 1925, in accordance with request made by self—Edgar Cayce.

PRESENT

Edgar Cayce; Morton H. Blumenthal, Conductor; Hugh Lynn Cayce, Steno. Mr. W. L. Jones.

READING

[254]

Time of Reading　　　　　　　　　　　　　　　*Southland Hotel,*
8:30 A.M.　　　　　　　　　　　　　　　　　*Norfolk, Virginia*

MHB: *Conditions surrounding Virginia Beach, in relation to the attempted establishment of the work, [900]'s relation to the work, what his interest should be towards same. Definite location of Plot 42. Conditions surrounding family and Virginia Beach.*

Mr. C: *As was and is, that in Plot 42 is on the way from Virginia Beach to North Virginia Beach. This is the place where the institution work should be established. It's just off of Seventeenth Street in Plot 42. Place of residence should be in North Virginia Beach, or Sea Pines. All conditions must be met for the good of the work. Choose the most acceptable place at present, for there will be many changes before being permanently established. The home and office will at present be located together. The establishment of the Institute will come about within three years. In the first year the lands necessary will be acquired, in the second year the foundations will be laid, the Institute will be complete by the end of the third year, Plot 42, just off Seventeenth Street.*

Then for the best works, find the most acceptable place, do the best under the present conditions.

Q-1. Give any information that will assist in becoming established at Virginia Beach.

A-1. First, locate the residence, getting in place as given. Then will come the means necessary for making the proper location. The Forces will provide same—indirectly. Then will come the outlay for the two parties interested. These two, [900] and Edgar Cayce. In the spring there will be two cottages, [900], Edgar Cayce and place of carrying on the work.

(Above) Because the Princess Anne Hotel seemed familiar, I selected it from an assortment of perhaps six other prominent Virginia Beach buildings of the period, all out of Norfolk's *The Ledgar-Star* newspaper files. By coincidence, three weeks later I was given the preceding aerial picture, wherein, almost dead center, there stood the very same hotel. (Reprinted from *Virginia Beach: A Pictorial History* by James M. Jordan IV and Frederick S. Jordan.) (Below) Despite its fuzziness and indications of fog that Virginia Beach never gets, this picture shows the beach boardwalk looking north from about 17th Street and what looks like a bingo tent at far left.

(Page 106) This first balloon aerial photograph shows Virginia Beach, circa 1925, just as the Cayce family found it on their arrival, which was by train and not by balloon. (Photograph by courtesy of Boice Studio, Virginia Beach, Virginia.)

(Above) Just as the 35th Street property appeared to the Cayces upon their arrival in September 1925. There doesn't seem to be an identity for the man coming around the east (left) side of the house. (Below) Even though the lawn needed mowing, the same place took on a whole new face after about two years (I'm presuming again), just by adding screens, a couple of planter boxes, planting lawn, and adding the 115 house number. Because the post office goofed in numbering the first three blocks from the ocean, possibly as it was the only house on the south side of the street, the number was eventually corrected to 315, and remains on the the same house today. Look carefully and you'll find two children behind the far left front screen.

Let me briefly preface the following few pages of verbatim readings extracts (because only the first one has been used in its entirety, while much has been deleted from the others—lack of space—after all, this is supposed to be a photographic publication), just so there is no misunderstanding about why I incorporated them into this compilation.

It is only my opinion, but I feel that these particular five readings are not only extremely pertinent to this portion of the book, they should be the most important basic readings to any individual having even remote influence upon the A.R.E. operation, which includes every employee, management directors and supervisors, Board of Trustees and President, and all voluntary entities.

Don't get me wrong! All of the Work Readings, these 254-series (there are 116—about 496 pages), are very important, but these are very basic ones, around which the Association will be built (it's still in its infancy) and operated.

[12/8/25 See 294-52 in re lack of funds, etc.]

WORK OF EDGAR CAYCE   **254-26**

This psychic reading given by Edgar Cayce at his office, 115 West 35th Street, Virginia Beach, Virginia, this 14th day of December, 1925, in accordance with request made by self—Edgar Cayce.

P R E S E N T

Edgar Cayce; Mrs. Cayce, Conductor; Gladys Davis, Steno.

R E A D I N G

[254]

Time of Reading   115 West 35th Street,
4:20 P.M. Eastern Standard   Virginia Beach, Va.

Mrs. C: *You will have before you the psychic work of Edgar Cayce, and all of those directly and indirectly associated and interested in same, and you will answer any questions that may be asked you regarding any or all of these. Should there be any questions asked here that should not be asked, you will please tell us so, and why.*

Mr. C: *Yes, we have the psychic phenomena as is manifested through Edgar Cayce. This we have had before, those that are interested directly and indirectly, and these are many, and there will be many more in the next few months. The ones directly interested in same and those directly associated with same should give out that information that would interest many more.*

Ready for the questions.

Q-1. It has often been given, in information from the psychic forces, (as manifested through Edgar Cayce) that at or near Virginia Beach, Virginia, was the place from which the phenomena should be propagated. Will you please tell us (since we are here), in an understandable manner to all present, why this is the place, and how the three directly associated with same should conduct themselves, physically, in respect to same.

A-1. There has been given as to why Virginia Beach, or near same, would be

109

the best place from which to propagate the work. That those present may better understand, we would then give same in this manner, for in same there is seen the action, physically also, of each that are directly associated with the phenomena as same operates, or the modus operandi of the action of the phenomena, see? The surrounding country is in that vibration as is a best predicated condition for the operation of psychic forces as may be manifested through this entity, from associations in the earth's plane and desires as are manifested through earthly forces, see? This applies as well to some of those associated with the work as to the individual through whom the operations are projected, see? The conditions that surround the place, Virginia Beach (not in its present season perhaps, as to the open knowledge of the individuals as are seen operating in this, but in the whole, and in the development of those conditions necessary for the establishment of an institution), are such that through same the phenomena might receive greater force and expansion. The nearness to the various ones directly interested in the propagation of the phenomena, see? The nearness (at another season than present) to the nation's and world's Capitol, that through same many channels of the thinking peoples who study such phenomena may have direct access to the phenomena, in a direct contactable manner, far from the real commercial influence of trade, that is of earthly commercial valuations. Near to sea, near to sands, near to many conditions that supply the greater forces for the easier accessibility of forces to phenomenize or materialize into the way and manner as may be more acceptable to the student, to the philosopher, to the theologian, to any of the cult, schism or ism, that might desire to study phenomena from the scientific angle, or from any *of the phases of the phenomena.*

As to, then, the conduct of those individuals associated with same, as this:

First, (this applying to all) in that manner, first, as will be wholly acceptable unto Him, the giver of all good and perfect gifts, as near as lies within the efforts of the physical bodies.

In the individual instances, as this:

For Edgar Cayce: Walk circumspectly before all men. Honest with self, with family, with associates, and let such honesty be the basis of all communications, with each and every individual, whether by word of mouth, by letter, by any accessible way of information being obtained or given from such forces—walk in that way, see. Ever remembering that the spirit of truth judgeth all things, and that man's conception of a truth is judged by the physical attributes or results from that attempted, in a material, in a moral, in a financial way and manner.

As to the director [Gertrude Cayce, Conductor]: in that way and manner that gives no false conception of the place occupied by the Director, or Interrogator, or in any way and manner that would divert any channel of assistance to any individual that would gain a better knowledge of the truth and Holy One, that may be phenomenized through the spirit of love, in the accessibility of truth as gained through such forces. In a way and manner that brings the greater respect of any who may contact such forces through the individuals themselves, see? for as is seen, each must be the truth, one toward another. [See Work: EC: Readings: Conduction.] [See 195-31, 6/8/26.]

As to the one that would give the message, as is taken [Gladys Davis, Steno.]: in earnest, in lowliness of spirit, in the way and manner knowing that the dependent one is in that obtained, see? for the correct manner of presentation may be often altered by the manner presented in type, see? and that too-sureness in self is often nearer in a way that does not give of the best in the projection of

110

truths as are presented; not of individual, but of the truth itself, see? [*See Work: EC: Readings: Stenographer.*]

Then as the combination again, these correlated in their efforts, in all then we find as these: As a unit, then, of strength. Let not there be brotherly strife (or sisterly *strife as would say in this case) in any way or manner, for in same there comes that not wholly circumspect in presentation of the best that lies in either.*

We are through for the present.

WORK OF EDGAR CAYCE   254-27

This psychic reading given by Edgar Cayce at his office, 115 West 35th Street, Virginia Beach, Virginia, this 19th day of December, 1925, in accordance with request made by self—Edgar Cayce.

. . . ready for questions.

Q-1. As given in former reading, the ones directly interested in same, and those directly associated with same, should give out that information that would interest many more. You will please tell us how the ones directly and indirectly associated should give out this information, and when.

A-1. Whenever possible. This, as we see, covers a vast scope of work, and of the exercising of the forces in the phenomena in various manners. As to giving same out, is a physical, mechanical, operation, for portions (any portions that may be chosen by the various ones directly associated with same) sent to those indirectly, or practically having little knowledge of same, would not only be of interest but would bring many more to the point of interest and in contact with same directly. Then, these things (as things, see?); that is, quotations from various readings, a compilation of truths as have been given in various phases of the work, should be compiled into pamphlets, books or leaflets, and first, beginning with the ones who have been indirectly associated or interested in the work, from the material or from a personal immaterial regarding work, these would form a nucleus to begin with, see? Then gradually expanding on this would bring a different phase and position, materially, to these operations. This is what is meant, and how. Begin, if only in a small way, to interest those in the various ways, see? [*1/16/26 & 3/15/27 See 195-21 & 195-41 in re pamphlet on EC work.*]

Q-2. What should Edgar Cayce, if anything, do in this and the adjoining vicinity to make known the work and his ideals in respect to same?

A-2. In the same vicinity, in the district, in the whole world, *distribute that as has been outlined here, see? Not as something emblazoned as something new; not as something as an idea; not as something as a mystery; not as something that is a side show—but rather as offering of self in service to him who would come, see?*

Q-3. How may the finances be obtained with which to have this literature printed and sent out?

A-3. This should be contributed by those directly interested in the propagation of same. Also by the work itself. That is, extracts from such will interest people who are willing to contribute, see? and there may be compiled data from same that would be acceptable to magazines and newspapers. These should be sent out, money received from same and expended in the expansion of the work.

Q-4. It has been given that when the work, or those associated with same were located at Virginia Beach, we should ask what should be done to obtain the finances necessary for the up-keep of the work and those associated with it. Also how to go about to establish an institution here. Will you now make this plain to us?

A-4. Many of the channels as have been given, we see, are open for this same, see? The forces are then the same—yesterday, today and forever—for these are of the making of the oneness of that force as may be manifested in the physical world from the oneness of all universal forces. Then, in this manner: First, as given, here, see? Virginia Beach. Then, begin in an honest, systematic manner to give to all directly and indirectly associated and interested in work the brief outline of the purpose and intent, and using then every channel through which means may be obtained to propagate such work, in the persistent, self-sacrificing, self-esteeming manner. Not as the beggar; not as one wantonly using the divine forces as are manifest in such phenomena, but as that of the right to use the forces in the way and manner as is commensurate with work or efforts of individuals applying same. Then, to newspapers, magazines, and to all of those channels through which data may be given and spread out to others, and through those channels as has been given that these forces may apply through this channel of supplying the needs for such an institute, see? Then, as we see, those various channels that offer assistance through the assistance lent in various manners, these too, as will be seen, will supply their portion. Such as is seen through the efforts of [137]—[900] in their operations and in their endeavors to understand the spiritual laws as are phenomenized in the material world and may be used in whole or part in their daily endeavors. Also in the articles or propaganda that may be ascribed to the efforts of either or both of these. Also in those efforts of [953] in the operations in the oil fields, as well as through those other channels, as is set by the individual, in the propagation of data as may be gathered from time to time. Also as may be seen in the efforts of [195] in the distribution of those properties that may prove of value to specific ills and ails of the human family, and in the association of the phenomena in other channels with the same individual work as is expanded from time to time. Also as is seen in the efforts of others that will come later in their various channels. Also as will be seen in the efforts of those in the next few months in the South, in the various channels and peoples that will become interested in the phenomena through [287] and also in the many various channels as are being opened by the partial efforts as expended, and which should be enlarged upon in the local or adjacent surroundings, to the present location. These then, all, in a systematic, in an honest applied effort by the individuals, in this way and manner may the propagation of the work be expanded, and may the institution receive that impetus as is necessary for the forwarding of same.

Yet all this must be done in that way and manner that gives all the glory and honor of same to that Holy One, the giver of all good and perfect gifts. Think not to bring self in that position as "I have accomplished, I will do," for the spirit of truth searcheth even to the joint and marrow, and the laws of the spiritual forces are even stricter than those of the secular as manifest in the physical, for in the manifesting of spiritual laws there is the oneness of the Father, made perfect in Him.

We are through for the present.

This psychic reading given by Edgar Cayce at his office, 115 West 35th Street, Virginia Beach, Virginia, this 18th day of February, 1926, in accordance with request made by self—Edgar Cayce.

PRESENT

Edgar Cayce; Mrs. Cayce, Conductor; Gladys Davis, Steno.

READING

[254]

Time of Reading   115 West 35th Street,
4:10 P.M. Eastern Standard   Virginia Beach, Va.

Mrs. C: *You will have before you the psychic work as done by Edgar Cayce, with the information as has been given regarding the locating of the work at Virginia Beach, Virginia. Now, it has been given that when Edgar Cayce was here we should ask questions concerning what should be done. Now, we would like to ask regarding property for Edgar Cayce and the Association. Also for those connected with same, especially Gladys Davis, and would ask that all information concerning same be given us at this time, giving any definite places that should be considered, and why, and you will answer any questions I will ask you.*

Mr. C: *Yes, we have the information as has been given through these forces regarding the psychic work and its propagation from Virginia Beach, Virginia.*

Now, as is seen in the study of the information as has been given, that, had that as given been followed out, there would have been sufficient means, through the natural *increase that has come to the property in the vicinity of Virginia Beach, for the full propagation of the work.*

Now, at the present time, with the body located near there, we find that the speculative interests in and about Virginia Beach are at their beginning, while there will be from fifty to a thousand percent advance in property in the various parts of the country adjacent to these lands. Then, as the speculative interest, this would then be good investment for anyone. As to specific places, as has been given, there will be many changes before the definite place is established; yet in any *place, even such as where the body is now located, would be* well, *and of the value that would in two years, see? be an advance of more than three times in value, and this then would be good as an investment, as well as a place to begin from.*

As to property for Association, as has been given, that along or near the outskirts or edge of the corporate limits, on or near 26th to 24th Street, extending toward the car line, see? Any of this would prove to be excellent property for such an institution, or any lying between North Virginia Beach and Cape Henry, in the edge of the sand hills.

As to property for those who may be interested in same, any that may be taken at the present prices even, of vacant property, may be of value as the increase speculation begins, for with the completion of the hotel resorts, and the playgrounds, there will be a large inflow of permanent and of winter transient, and this will enhance the values and will bring large returns on investments.

As to that of the specific nature, as regarding Gladys Davis, we find there has much been given as respecting this, but with the general information as given, it will be seen that the value of property will increase. Then why not take advantage of same?

As to questions regarding the work and its development, the prices as are quoted are apparently high, yet, as has been given, these will increase for the next thirty to forty years in value, as has been given, see?

Ready for questions.

Q-1. Would it be well, then, that Gladys Davis consider purchasing the place or the house she looked at today on 24th Street?

A-1. Answer self, from that as given.

Q-2. Which would be the better place for Edgar Cayce to consider—the place he occupies at present or the house and lot he looked at this morning on 24th Street?

A-2. The one on 35th Street will advance forty percent to the other ten.

Mrs. C: *That is all the questions.*

WORK OF E.C.
VIRGINIA BEACH

This psychic reading given by Edgar Cayce at his office, 115 West 35th Street, Virginia Beach, Virginia, this 26th day of February, 1926, in accordance with request made by [900].

. . . ready for questions.

Q-1. What price should be offered for the house and lot at 115 35th Street —and when?

A-1. $11,500, to $12,500, and the sooner this is accomplished the better, for we will find, as the season advances, there will be advance in price.

Q-2. Do we understand that the advance in the price of this of 40% will be from this price?

A-2. We will find that within two-and-a-half years this will advance more than 40% from $13,000. Yes, it may be sold for $20,000 in 1927–8.

Q-4. When should this be bought?

A-4. As given, this will be found to advance as the season advances, and there will be a great deal more speculation in Virginia Beach and vicinity property in the next two years than even at the present season or year, see? While these will continue to advance, and while the properties are exorbitant in price, apparently, the season, the place, as we will see, will bring many dollars and many peoples to this vicinity, and as has been given aforetime, much of the land in various quarters will bring high prices, see? Hence, there may be much money made in any lands, especially in the vicinity as given, see? for with the building of the central portion or business section, and with the building of year-round resorts, there will be the joining of many enterprises that will make this, Virginia Beach, Virginia, an exceptional place, see? for investments, for the next three to five years especially, and the sooner this is now purchased the more advantageous will be the prospects for such advances, see?

Q-5. How soon should this be sold?

A-5. Not under two years.

Q-6. What portions of Virginia Beach will build the faster?

A-6. That from 40th and 50th Street to the southernmost end at present, and **254-29** *then extending along the Norfolk Boulevard, see?*

Q-7. Should the land for the Institute be purchased at this time? If so, where?

A-7. Between 26th–24th Streets, as given, or between 26th and 27th—the higher ground, see? The sooner the better.

Now, there may be much information given regarding the conditions as surround this place as a resort, for with the changes as are coming over the various places along the Atlantic Seaboard, and with the advertising that is being done, and as has been contemplated and will be added more and more, we find that now more local interest is being created. This will, of its own self, create more outside influence, and as the natural conditions *surround the place of many historic natures, this, as we see, gives the greater impetus to the improvements as will be made from time to time, and the sooner this becomes more of an all-year-round resort, the more improvements will naturally be shown, see? and the greater numbers that come, the greater becomes the opportunities in all branches, for there are many various branches of industries of various natures, and businesses, that will be established in and near Virginia Beach.*

We are through for the present.

This psychic reading given by Edgar Cayce at his office, 115 West 35th Street, **254-31** *Virginia Beach, Virginia, this 25th day of August, 1926, in accordance with request made by Edgar Cayce.*

PRESENT

Edgar Cayce; Mrs. Cayce, Conductor; Gladys Davis, Steno.
Dr. & Mrs. T. B. House, and Hugh Lynn Cayce

READING

[254] (WORK)

Respecting individual association with the psychic work, we find this is as varied as individuals, yet each, that is already or may become associated with same, will find those words of the apostle to the Master—that each may present their bodies a living sacrifice, which is a reasonable service. To some there has been given the ability to serve as prophets; some as teachers; some as ministers; some in one manner, some in another; which are spiritual gifts, and of the same source, when applied in that manner that brings service to the fellow man; for in sending the Son into the world, as flesh, becoming the Son of Man, man's service to God becomes then fellow service to fellow man, and through same exemplifying God's gift to the world. . . .

In the manner *of conducting such work, there is seen there have been times when there seems to have been evil done that good might come from same. Oft will it be learned, by the study of phenomena of people's actions, that seemingly all forces in the universe are used to bring about that which is good, for it has been said, "I will harden the heart of pharaoh, that he will not let my children go." Through this same seed came the Son of Man, and through these same trials through which the forefathers passed, the burdens and sins of the world were laid upon that Son.*

115

Then, through the trials, the temptations, the besetters of evil from within and from without, may any work that is His (God's) be expected to grow, and in that manner become polished bright, and a shining light unto the world; yet though He were the Son, He learned obedience through the things which He suffered.

In the individual association, then, we find there are many already associated, in one direction or another. Each have their individual work with same to accomplish—some as teachers, some as ministers, some as directors, some in one channel, some in another.

Ready for questions.

Q-1. Should the Institute be begun on a small scale at first?

A-1. From acorns great oaks grow. The Son of Man was the Babe in the Manger. The beginning of all great institutions, of all great things, is first in the mind of individuals who are in touch with infinite forces. "The silver and the gold is mine," saith the Lord. Begin—as was given to the prophet of old—"What hast thou in hand?" and this same rod, cast before Pharaoh, brought the plagues to the nation. The same spread over the sea divided same. The same brought consternation when smiting the rock, and said, "Shall I (not shall God) give to this stubborn and stiff-necked people?"

Then, use that thou hast in hand, in the direction in which same may be applied in that same way and manner, that the great aid, succor, and help, may be given to the mental and the body deficiency, and that the ways of the wicked may be pointed out, and that many may find the Lord—for He is not afar off, but dwells within thine own heart. "This day I have set before thee good and evil. Choose thou" whom thy peoples, thy mind, thy body, will serve; for, as has been given, "I present my body a living sacrifice, which is a reasonable service."

Q-2. Would it be to the best interest of the work for Edgar Cayce to make a trip to Florida to obtain finances for the Institute?

A-2. There has been given—even as reference has been made here—that seemingly, ofttimes the wicked are used to further good. Through these channels the first large amounts may be obtained for the beginning of such work. The conditions to be considered, rather, are those individuals to whom such finances would be committed for expenditure—in that way and manner of serving mankind, through and in that channel as been said shall be the criterion of every individual seeking to serve through such a way and manner. Some as have been chosen, or spoken of, are. Others are not—yet their willingness to serve is as the beginning of wisdom for many.

In the numbers, we would give such as these should be the ones to serve:

[900] should direct that that shall be given as a message to the world, and to individuals.

Edgar Cayce should direct that manner of the approach to each individual's place of service in such an institution, through the same sources through which this information is given—choosing, then, no one, without first consulting, as it were, those forces.

As given, Thomas Burr House may direct that manner of applying to the physical body-physical conditions for the benefit of the physical functioning of that body.

Others may be chosen in the same way and manner.

116

the beginning of the Institute.

A-3. As has oft been given, ask and you shall receive. From those who have received benefits should first come that nucleus, about which there would be many that would add thereto. As credence is gained, as the material benefits are derived, then that as is necessary for the material portion will be supplied, provided *all is done in the way and manner as here given, and has oft been given. Let each work in this manner: "May the words of my mouth, the meditation of my heart, the deeds of my hands, the thoughts and expression of my mind, be acceptable in thy sight, my Lord, my redeemer."*

In the first, as has been given, the individual or initial sum may be obtained through the Florida connection. Much more may be gained through New York connection—as Lauterstein, Levy, Bergeson [?], Kraus, Bernstein [?],* and March. . . .

Q-6. When would be the best time for Edgar Cayce to make the trip to Florida or New York?

A-6. When the men ask to see him, and to come.

Q-7. You will give any general advice to those associated with the work that will assist them in any way.

A-7. Each—each—each—shall approach that source of advice in their own concept of service desired to be rendered. Not that the individual should give another individual their concept of what the other thinks, or how desires the other to serve God. Let this mind be in each that would associate, or that would serve: This is my *work in a manner as attempting to better serve my fellow man, in understanding the issues of life, and my association, my brother's association and relation to his Creator. . . .*

Q-9. What course should Edgar Cayce pursue to bring [900] and Mr. [953] to cooperate better regarding the work?

A-9. Let each ask that they may serve together, in better cooperation, and there will be given, through these sources, the way, the manner, the position, each would serve the better. There has been given to each that they, each, as individuals, have a portion, a part, a service to render. Let each desire to cooperate in such service, for each may be sure that each man is held responsible or accountable for the deeds and the thoughts done in the body.

The same may be said of each individual who already would serve. Let each seek to serve, and the position, the conditions surrounding same, will be given, and these may be very sure.

Q-10. Would Mr. Van Patten of Virginia Beach be the correct one for the secretary of the Institute?

A-10. Correct, if he will apply himself to those same conditions as have been given, for the abilities of the body lie within self to be made compatible to those things as have been set forth. Associations socially, financially, and mentally, of the individual are peculiarly fitted for same, if he will apply them.

Q-11. What other individuals in Virginia Beach or Norfolk should be approached by Edgar Cayce?

A-11. As has been given, individuals must first seek that they be of service. Service rarely seeks individuals. God has given every man his abilities. Man seeks to apply same to God's service. This is God's work.

Mrs. C: *That is all the questions.*

Mr. C: *There may be much said respecting individuals, and association*

[* See pp. 51–52 Stearn's book, *A Door To the Future.*]

and cooperation, and as to how each, as individuals, or as cooperating individuals, may apply themselves.

Then, seek more often that counsel as may be received through Him that would give all unto those who serve.

We are through.

[Association of National Investigators, Incorporated, was incorporated on May 6, 1927.]

This psychic reading given by Edgar Cayce at his office, 115 West 35th Street, Virginia Beach, Virginia, this 4th day of June, 1927, in accordance with request made by those present.

PRESENT

Edgar Cayce; [900], Conductor; Gladys Davis, Steno.
Mrs. Edgar Cayce and Huge Lynn Cayce, Mrs. Morton Blumenthal, and Mr. & Mrs. David E. Kahn.

READING

[254]

Time of Reading
6:10 P.M. Eastern Standard Time

115 West 35th Street,
Virginia Beach, Va.

[900]: *Now, you will have before you the Association of National Investigators, Inc., as formed today. You will tell us if it has been formed in the correct manner—how to proceed in this matter; tell us where the hospital should be located that this Association is to conduct; tell us if the Board of Trustees are correct and legally instituted, and how we may the better proceed to carry out our purpose. You will give this advice; give us practical guidance, and answer questions regarding this matter. You will also have before you all those connected with the work.*

Mr. C: *Yes, we have the association as has been incorporated. These conditions surrounding same we have had before. The legal phases, so far, have been attended to in a proper way and manner. The trustees as have been endowed with the power to transact the business of same, as a whole, are very good. There are some whose names appear that are not, as yet, wholly in accord with the work being attempted. These should not be discarded, but rather disregarded, until such a time that they—through the exercising of those forces as have been set in motion—are in accord with the work being attempted.*

There are many things, many conditions, to be considered as respecting the next steps that should be considered. Especially should all those be considered who have—through their effort, and through their work—contributed to that as necessary to bring to the lives of others that necessary influence to have made such work possible.

Those things as concern each individual should be set forth in the literature that may be sent to all such individuals; for many will be interested—many

118

the ark.

As to those conditions that next should be considered—first that of the policy of the Association, which is set forth in the charter granted—purely a philanthropic work, and not for personal gain, other than edification to self and others.

The next step—first that of the notification to all who have been interested in the phenomena and perfecting the organization, and the necessary action on the part of each and every individual to become a member of Association and participate in the benefits of the study as is to scientifically be made as respecting the good that may be gained from such phenomena for the benefit of all concerned. See?

The next step—the classification of the memberships of such an organization. First to be considered is that as may be called the lay member, or one who is seeking for the physical relief for self—or loved one—through the sources as may be supplied by and through the efforts of the Association. Next those who, through their own act, may contribute such an amount as to make it possible for those who are not financially able to gain such knowledge, or such association, through the regular channels, may have benefit of such.

Third, those that would act as those members of committee, or work as a group towards the perfecting of those plans as may bring into existence the actual building and the actual outlay of the work.

Ready for questions.

Q-1. In order to prevent—in some future time—some more material minded person taking advantage of the prosperity this corporation may enjoy, how may we so protect the corporation, and how may we provide for the possible dissolution of the corporation, and the distribution of any equity remaining to the corporation?

A-1. In this there are many conditions to be considered. First, there should not be a trustee appointed or elected unless the association of the entity, in the whole earth experience, is in keeping with the purpose of the organization. If the tend, bend, trend, of an individual is correct, *and the association has been such as to make same in keeping with the intent of the present, all well. Do not elect such a one until their life experience in the earth's plane is in keeping. Hence there is given, there are those not in accord—for, as is seen and as given, legally the intent and purpose of the organization is set forth correct. Keep same correct, by and through that intent and purpose for which it is set. Then the forces do not defeat their own purpose. . . .*

Q-3. Regarding the initial membership fee—in taking into consideration the number of readings given, or possible to be given, and all other considerations, which would be most beneficial to the corporation—a $20 or $30 initial fee?

A-3. Not which is most beneficial to corporation, but which is most in keeping with that intent and purpose for which corporation is set. Twenty—for in this we find in keeping with those numbers as are set in purpose; for two and naught is as an initial entrance into that of the days as are set for man's existence in an experience. Explain same? As this:

We find that in this number there is that which prevents the ones who through that of purely the seeker for only personal interests would be loath to part, and he who is able to contribute little may not be hindered by same, see? Hence, as has been given, give all those who have had any association with the work, or the phenomena, that opportunity to still be identified with same. Send them, then, this as the letter:

"To those who have been interested, directly or indirectly, in the phenomena as has been manifested through Mr. Cayce, these come as greetings. There has been perfected the Association of National Investigators, Incorporated. This as the way for the more efficient study of the phenomena, that it may supply through same the benefits that mankind in general may gain through same. This is to ask, then—that should you desire to gain an access to the study as is being made by this Association—for you to become a member of such an Association; for being limited in the amount of work that may be given, the readings may be had only by such members. The membership fee for those that have already had readings is $15. For those who are members, readings may be given at the nominal sum of $10." See? . . .*

Q-12. Should we not build a hospital immediately—but rather start with the operating, or rather with the educational end?

A-12. Begin with the hospital, but build first around the lecture and library— but build the hospital, for first, as the Master gave, those were the lessons as were given to the individuals—to heal the physical, and thus gain a knowledge of that necessary. For the Master built no churches—but He laid the foundation. The foundations have been laid in that as has been given, and the manner is set forth here. Proceed! Go! Begin! Now! Let the plans be drawn. Let the work begin— and would those for secular reasons gain materially, gain control of the lands nearby! for these will prove valuable!

Q-13. Will you give me advice and guidance now of anything further that I may do?

A-13. There has been placed, my son, in thine hands, again, that of the position of the counsellor to many peoples, and as there is gathered about thee those who labored with and against thee—yet for that one purpose as was to unify the knowledge that man in this mundane sphere might have as respecting those Creative Forces as are manifest in the material world—keep thine self in that way that will ever keep the face of those who seek Him toward the light; for the light is set in Him, and thou art chosen as a vessel for that light. Be not broken on the wheel of strife, nor yet be thou over-anxious—for these are but the wayside of those who would be led astray. Keep the counsel of Him who gave that, "Come unto me and I will make thy burden light, for my yoke is easy—but learn of me."

Keep thy paths straight, and let others know that there is set in Israel a light that will draw all men unto Him; for even as the serpent was raised in the wilderness for the healing of the people, even may that institution, and those as are gathered with thee, be raised as a light that will bring healing to the ones who will look on His face, and gain the knowledge of self, as may be applied toward that directing way.

Keep thine self unspotted from the world, for thy way is not an easy way; yet there is peace, joy, and that as the inner knowledge of a life being spent in building for those who seek His face. All is well!

We are through.

120

(Above) Looking north northwest from the front steps of 315 35th Street, where Gertrude Cayce sits (right), one would have seen open country-side like this, with only two houses in sight. However, just out of the picture in right background would be portions of the Cavalier Hotel (still there today, but empty) along with numerous summer houses along the Atlantic Ocean beach front. Now, it's solid with houses, apartments, churches, highrise hotels, and condominiums lining the waterfront. Those are the Cayce brothers above, while (right) Gertrude may be wondering if those milk bottles will be noticed and cause curiosity, because of the late afternoon sunshine.

(Below) Gertrude Cayce at the wheel, would do much of the family driving chores in coming years.

121

(Right) While his brother, Edwin, was hesitant, Morton H. Blumenthal got his feet wet first . . . that is, he found Edgar Cayce first through David E. Kahn early in the less-than-two-year stay the Cayces had in Dayton. It was Morton who stimulated greater emphasis on dreams and obtained many reading interpretations of his own dreams, practically on a daily basis. These dreams directed him into Christian faith, closer association with the Cayce family, and even involvement in sponsoring the Edgar Cayce work in Virginia Beach. Much of the dream research, the educational program of A.R.E. today, is based on philosophical information that Morton and his brother sought through the readings. They founded Atlantic University.

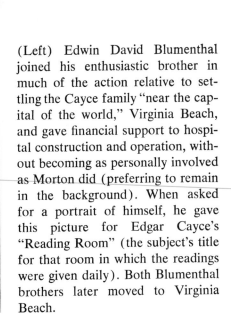

(Left) Edwin David Blumenthal joined his enthusiastic brother in much of the action relative to settling the Cayce family "near the capital of the world," Virginia Beach, and gave financial support to hospital construction and operation, without becoming as personally involved as Morton did (preferring to remain in the background). When asked for a portrait of himself, he gave this picture for Edgar Cayce's "Reading Room" (the subject's title for that room in which the readings were given daily). Both Blumenthal brothers later moved to Virginia Beach.

Edgar Cayce poses, hat in hand, on his daily inspection tour of the hospital construction, wherein he would often pitch in with hammer and nails to help things along (Hugh Lynn says his father was a capable carpenter).

Then (below), with the exterior completed, we view the hospital and garage from two different angles, showing the landscaping work underway and 67th Street (it was 105th Street then) being graded by horse-drawn scarifing equipment and far enough along for automobile traffic.

Looking slightly northwest down along the hospital front entrance porch, it's possible to distinguish outlines of a summer house through the end archway. The photographer adjusted his exposure for the available light on the porch and lost all detail of the outdoor surroundings. (Below) I suppose this was called the living room, but it has been the reception lobby of A.R.E. Headquarters since 1956.

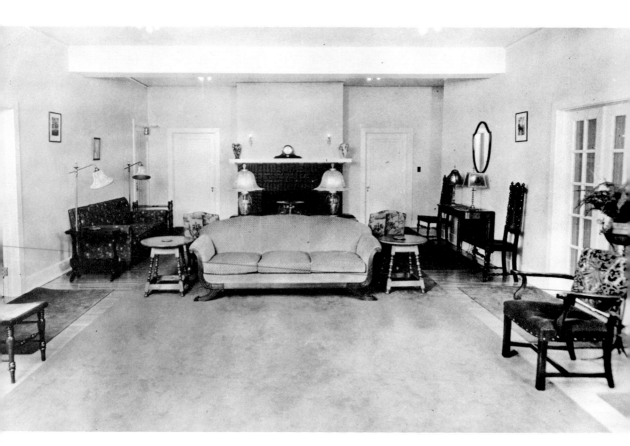

(Above) Of the original three wards like this, the fourth floor now utilizes one as an apartment and meeting place for the Prayer Group, another for the Braille Library, and the third houses the Editorial Department. Prior to 1970 they served as dormitory sleeping quarters, along with four or five private rooms on the third floor, for registered symposium/seminar guests, who were fed in the cafeteria dining area below, which you see here as the Cayce Hospital dining room (below). If you look carefully (above) you will see the reflected image of the photographer and his flash in that dresser mirror at the right hand side of the picture. The A.R.E. Book Room occupied the former cafeteria dining area below, from 1970 until 1975. Only the living room area was changed much.

(Above) Hugh Lynn Cayce talked of his father's strange abilities to his college room-mate, Thomas Sugrue, so much that Tom came with him to Virginia Beach intent upon proving the clairvoyant a fake. Instead, he had readings, was put on a re-search committee with Gladys and Hugh Lynn, and later became editor of the first journal. *Portrait © Underwood & Underwood.* (Right) Gladys Davis poses her-self comfortably for this picture on the Cayce's front steps plateau . . . a most "fetching" scene.

On the beach two blocks from the hospital or Cayce house, we find (left to right) Dr. Thomas B. and Carrie Salter House (how about those bathing caps?) In front of them is Anne Elizabeth Gray, then Ecken, Jack Sawyer, and Cayces—Gertrude and Edgar. All pose self-consciously, especially Edgar, looking like the cameraman had asked him to move closer to Gertrude. All of the kids and Edgar appear to have come directly from the water.

THE SELMA TIMES-JOURNAL
Tuesday, July 24, 1928

HOSPITAL NAMED FOR FORMER SELMIAN AS REWARD FOR LABORS

A dream come true, is the way Selma friends of Edgar Cayce, former photographer and psychic of this city, are commenting on news of the recent award of a contract for $100,000 for erection of a 30 bed hospital to be called the Cayce Hospital, at Virginia Beach, Va., by the National Association of Investigators, Inc., of which Mr. Cayce is secretary-treasurer, for the practical application of psychical aid to the sick.

Cayce had the dream during his 13 years residence in Selma. He left this city in 1924 for Dayton, Ohio, to continue his work as a psychic, becoming an officer of the National Investigation, Inc., of which Morton Blumenthal, New York millionaire, is president. Mr. Cayce desired to place the hospital in Alabama at that time.

The Virginia Beach, Va., Weekly, in commenting on the construction of the Cayce Hospital in a front page article sets forth the excellent plan for the structure, which is the first unit of a much larger institution which the organization intends to erect. The site is the highest elevation between Cape Henry and the Beach, commanding a magnificent view of a wide territory. Rudolphe, Cooke and Van Leeuweon are architects and contractors are the United Construction Company. Concrete foundations of the building are under way.

Says the Virginia Beach Exchange: "The Association of National Investigators was incorporated May 6, 1927 in the State of Virginia. Although founded upon the psychic work of Mr. Edgar Cayce and although the immediate basis of its foundation was to further foster and encourage the psychical, mental and spiritual benefits that thousands are deriving from Mr. Cayce's endeavors in the psychic field, nevertheless the larger and more embracing purpose of the organization is to enlarge psychic research and also to provide for the practical application of any [research].

THE VIRGINIA BEACH WEEKLY
Friday, July 20, 1928

CONSTRUCTION ON CAYCE HOSPITAL UNDERWAY COST IS $100,000

BUILDING IS SITUATED HIGH ON SAND DUNE NEAR 105TH ST.
IS FIRST UNIT, OTHERS MAY BE ADDED.

The National Association of Investigators has let a contract for the construction of a thirty bedroom hospital at Virginia Beach. The new building will be known as the Cayce Hospital For Research and Enlightment and is of concrete and shingle construction, four stories in height. Besides the thirty bedrooms, it will contain a large lobby and dining room, a lecture hall, library, doctors' quarters and spacious porches.

The total cost of the investment, including ground, building and equipment will be approximately $100,000. Plans for the structure were drawn by Rudolph, Cooke and Van Leeuween and the contract awarded to the United Construction Company of Norfolk. Rapid progress has been made during the past two weeks, the concrete foundation walls being almost completed.

The site of the hospital will be one of its most attractive features. Rising from a high sand dune, probably the highest elevation between Cape Henry and the Beach, it commands a view of the territory for many miles around. The property measures 150 by 300 feet along 105th Street and extends between Holly Avenue and the boulevard. The present building is the first unit and will be followed by others as the occasion demands.

The Association of National Investigators was incorporated May 6th, 1927, in the State of Virginia. Although founded upon the psychic work of Mr. Edgar Cayce, and although the immediate basis of its formation was to further foster and encourage the physical, mental and spiritual benefit that thousands have and are deriving from Mr. Cayce's endeavors in the psychic field, nevertheless, the larger and more embracing purpose of the organization is to engage in general psychic research and also to provide for the practical application of any knowledge obtainable through the medium of psychic phenomena. In the matter of specific application, the Association seeks to render physical aid to the sick and ailing through its hospital, and also to disseminate and exploit for the good of humanity knowledge obtained from its research work through the lecture hall, library and other educational channels.

The Association Hospital will furnish those who seek physical readings and desire to secure treatment exactly as prescribed therein, the opportunity to gain same at the hands of competent and sympathetic physicians. The hospital is to be conducted along only the most modern, scientific, as well as ethical lines. Every comfort and service for room, board and treatment will be such as is customary to an institution of this kind, and all moneys so paid except the physicians' fees will go towards its maintenance.

P R E S E N T

Edgar Cayce; Morton Blumenthal, Conductor; Gladys Davis, Steno.
Mrs. Edgar Cayce, Hugh Lynn Cayce, Mr. L. B. Cayce, Thomas B. House, Jr.,
and Dr. Thos. B. House.

R E A D I N G

[254]

Time of Reading
12:45 A.M. Eastern Standard Time.

Mr. B: *You will have before you the work of the Association of National Investigators, Inc., and the Board of Directors governing same. You will direct this Board, both individually, in regard to each individual's relation to it, and collectively, in regard to the responsibility of the Board in this undertaking of the Association. You will instruct Blumenthal and Kahn, and Wyrick, and Bradley, and Brown, and Cayce, and each of the rest, just what it is that the Forces seek the Association to materialize in the work that the Forces seek to accomplish through the Association. You will then answer questions that I will ask you regarding it.*

Mr. C: *Yes, we have those conditions, aims, purposes, and the work as set forth in that which has been termed Association of National Investigators, Incorporated, with its officers, and that which should be accomplished through these channels.*

It has been given, in that which has been maintained in information supplied concerning such an association, the aims, the endeavors, and that which should be accomplished in same. Much may be said pertaining to the work to be accomplished, and many various phases of same are then to be considered, would the greater work, the greater efforts, be expended in the work of the Association.

Its aim, its purpose as set forth and given, is correct; for it, the work, that accomplished, is to be first of all an educational factor in the lives of those that are contacted through the efforts of the Association. This pertaining to the physical, the mental, and the spiritual—for, as given, these and their relations to one another are the primary forces in the physical or material life. The greater understanding of the relationship of these factors, and that the whole is one, yet must be studied in their individual, *and collective, and coordinating influence in the lives of individuals—and, as given, first to the individual, then to groups, to classes, to masses. This, then, is the work to be accomplished by the Association.*

In the efforts of the Board, then:

First there must be wholehearted cooperation; all of one mind, and that mind to serve in the fullest sense in the dissemination of that gained through the sources of the Association work and its application in the physical, the mental, and the spiritual life of its members. Again, without that wholehearted cooperation and oneness of mind and purpose, irrespective of position, condition, relation one with another, there may not be expected the result desired; any more than of a misdirected mind attempting to understand a spiritual law through a purely physical application, or a physical law by spiritual application; for the spiritual is the life; *the mental is the* builder; *the physical is the* result. *This, then, should be first and foremost: The determined purpose of the Board to have wholehearted cooperation, in a one-minded purpose, and that purpose to make manifest the love of God and man; man's relation to man; man's relation to God. In* this *there must come, as has ever been given, success in such terms as the service is meted; and there may be expected that wholehearted cooperation from the divine, in the mental and the* purely material, *in the same relation as the whole-heartedness is to the oneness of purpose! A divided house* cannot *stand.*

As to those individual relationships:

There has been chosen a Board, of and for same. There has been materially set forth, in a manner, the office of each. Wholehearted cooperation, then, in each—not only *in its specified office or duty—can bring* only *wholehearted cooperation in its biggest, broadest, and better sense. This* is just plain common sense. . . .

So, as may be said of each and every individual as may be associated, as an officer or as a member of such work; for in this there must stand first and foremost that the directing of self in the inner man must be made in oneness of purpose, as of the truth set forth in the purpose, the aim, of the association or organization. For when they all labored with one accord, and were of one mind, there was added daily such as would receive the word of truth that made men free! Ready for questions.

Q-1. What should the name of the hospital be? since the name of the Association represents our entire institution?

A-1. Hospital of the Association, or Cayce Hospital of Enlightenment and Investigation, or Hospital for Enlightenment of those seeking truth.

Q-2. Any one of these names?

A-2. In choosing names, names may, or may not, mean anything, *to individuals. To others, it means much. This, the Association hospital, will* only *be known by one name—that of the one whose dream such has been, and it will be called by that name, and in the succeeding generations, as thought is turned into those channels, the same will be as that in the beginning; for, as seen, none are being drawn into that purpose of the establishing of this more close relation of God's truth in earth—through spiritual understanding of spiritual things, mental application of mental building, or the material through which both manifest— other than those that first established same in that land now known as Egypt. In that beginning, there were those gathered (as here), in various offices, various positions. As each bore their relation to the peoples of that period, each in the present relation bears that relation to the peoples according to their individual development, plus that as the desire to make manifest that so builded in that momentous period in man's understanding. In that known at that period; we find each bearing that relation to that being attempted to be disseminated by those who were the founders of same. This relation existed:*

When there was the first entrance into this land by the peoples from the north country, and the man—[165] subduing those peoples—set self up as the ruler of same, there came that conviction in self—through that witnessed by that body—of those conditions which were being experienced by the peoples of the land subdued. [900], then, was among those subdued, and the teacher, and giving to the peoples those of the mysticism of numbers, of the relationship of the stars, of those as were later depicted in many of the characters as became the

there came the conviction of the king to pit the abilities of his son against the son of the native's, and the son then was set in rule as that of Araaraart (or [341] in the present). These pitted, then, as to their abilities to give to the peoples the better understanding of the mystic or mysterious forces as were made, and as are *made, manifest in, then and now called, nature or natural forces.*

In the choosing of the ones to lead, such counsellors were chosen among the peoples of the land—both native and of those brought in. Among those we find many in the present Board, as seen—[195], [953], [900]—and others that will *be interested later.*

The choosing of the leader [294] in the one set as priest, this became a momentous question—as to who should be chosen. And when this was first set up, there arose many dissensions, that—in the division which afterward arose— became as minor or major rebellions during a physical existence. In the return, in the again establishing of this priest, in the minor position, yet through the establishing of the priest arose that which became that study as is being founded *this day, in a distant land—yet nigh unto those same shores that washed the shores of the lands of that land—and these call from, and for, the forces of all* to *harken unto that as is being accomplished! Then, in the activities of those, there arose much, many, and heaps of those same tenets as were given by Him Who first gave, "The meek shall inherit the earth."*

Those are the tenets upon which this *foundation must be laid. In that name, and in Him, shall many find blessings and understandings.*

Q-3. **What shall be inscribed upon the cornerstone of the building?**

A-3. *Build this in the triangle, and this shall be the inscription: Cayce Hospital—Research and Enlightenment—founded by (the next stone) Association of National Investigators, Inc., 1927. (The next) That we may make manifest the love of God and man.*

Virginia Beach (Virginia) *Weekly,*
November 9, 1928

Cayce Hospital To Be Dedicated Armistice Day

Building Four Stories High Containing 30 Bedrooms. Cost Approx. $150,000

The Cayce Hospital on 105th Street near Atlantic Boulevard at Virginia Beach is now nearing completion and will be formally dedicated on Armistice Day, Sunday, November 11th. The building which when completed will cost approximately $150,000 with furnishings has been under construction since last June. The public is invited to attend the exercises which will take place at 1:30 p. m.

Dr. William M. Brown, of the department of psychology and education at Washington and Lee University will make the dedicatory address. Morton Blumenthal, of New York, president of the Association of National Investigators, and Dr. Edgar Cayce, the secretary, are also on the program for addresses.

The Hospital has been established by the association and is the only intitution of its kind in the world, being wholly devoted to the study of psychical research and the effect of psychical phenomena on physical ills. It is based upon the studies of Dr. Cayce, who has been engaged in the work for the past thirty years.

New York *American,* October 22, 1928

NEW PSYCHIC HOSPITAL TO FIND AILMENTS

Offers Diagnosis of Physical Troubles by Mental Method, Even to Absentee Patients

A group of American men and women, including three New Yorkers, have made an endowment of over $100,000 for a "psychic" hospital, the first of its kind to be built in America. Ailments of the body will be diagnosed at the hospital by means of psychic concentration. It will not be necessary for patients to be at the hospital for "readings" They may be thousands of miles away and still be diagnosed.

The hospital, to be known as the Cayce Hospital for Research and Enlightment, will be formally opened November 11 at Virginia Beach, Va. Two of the three New York sponsors are Morton H. Blumenthal, a broker of No. 50 Broadway, and David E. Kahn, of the furniture industry.

NAMED FOR INVESTIGATOR.

At his office last night Mr. Blumenthal explained that the hospital was named after Edgar Cayce, known by many for his probings into the subconscious.

(Above) Leslie B. ("Squire") Cayce without a doubt was discussing opening ceremonies for Cayce Hospital with Linden Shroyer at 35th Street, while Dr. Thomas B. House watched from behind them. (Right, above) Perhaps someone of importance was late for dedication ceremonies, causing that disgruntled expression on Edgar's face, and the Squire looks as though he's expecting his son to blow his cork. They are in the porte-cochere at the rear of the hospital. (Right, below) Dr. Thomas B. House seated at his desk in his hospital office.

(Above) Attempts to lighten deep, early-morning, winter shadows, cast by tall pine trees along the south side of 67th Street, may be visible in the finished halftone, but restoration wasn't simple. It is my theory that the landscape contractor snapped this picture, possibly to show that he did actually use wooden forms for pouring the six concrete lampposts. (Below) I did that black rectangular overlay to outline the area of this fine professional photograph chosen to appear in a folded Christmas greeting that, after retouching and printing procedures, was mailed to former hospital patients in 1929.

THE
NEW TO-MORROW

Published Quarterly by The Association of National Investigators, Inc.

For Its Members

Publication Office—*Virginia Beach, Va.*

Editorial Office—*Lexington, Va.*

THOMAS J. SUGRUE, *Editor*   HUGH LYNN CAYCE, *Managing Editor*

VOL. 1   DECEMBER, 1929   No. 1

Contents

Thomas Sugrue had not begun working on *There Is a River* at this point; another book by him was to be published before the Edgar Cayce story. However, as you will notice (above) he was kept fairly busy with editorial chores on the Association of National Investigators' (Incorporated) first journal, the predecessor to the *A.R.E. Journal* published at this time. Actually, it was a larger publication, but the contents page was reduced to fit here.

This is one of those times when I felt that only a small portion of a particular reading was all that was necessary to explain the situation. You have the privilege of looking up the whole reading if your curiosity is getting to you. You live where! If you're an A.R.E. member you can buy the whole set of Work Readings.

7th day of March, 1929

Q-11. Regarding the plans discussed by [195] and [900] for the establishment of a college at Virginia Beach, are these realizable?

A-11. Realizable, plausible, feasible—and not only this. These may, through their fullness of purport, gain for themselves and millions of others such a center, such an institution. The Association of Learning, in the field that would bring the more perfect understanding for self and for others.

Q-12. Are we not right in formulating plans first to appropriate ten million dollars, to be obtained from the machine,* for the university, and secondly to make the university a university in every sense of the word—

A-12. Absolutely correct! and would be maintained through the very phases of the phenomena *as would bring, and will bring about, the more perfect understanding of the universality of force through the very channels that would bring the* material *means for such an undertaking.*

Q-13. When should we just begin to—

A-13. At once in mind, for Mind is ever the Builder—and as these are builded in the mental forces of the individual there is added to same the abilities of all the cosmic *forces as would see such an undertaking realized; which has been the* dream *of all—and had any of the teachers established such, how vast the difference in the world's map!*

Q-14. Now we plan various buildings to take each its own branch—one the psychic phenomena and spiritual kind of philosophy, the other the college for cultural subjects, the other the business building—are the various names for the buildings and the general plan as I dream it one well to work out? for given the material means there's no question as to whether I will put it through, if I get the Lord's help—

A-14. Then keep the Lord on thy side, my son, and these may come to pass, even as visioned, dreamed, they may be made material conditions in thine own experience.

Q-15. Would next year—will it prove a good time to found the college?

A-15. Read that was given thee as would come in thine endeavors in that of the second year from 1929, or that would come to thee in '31 and 2, and there will be seen that already there has been set the calling for thee in such an undertaking, and indeed would there be a message for mine people who have long remained in bondage through superstition and through dogmatic relations as have been brought about by those that would teach "as I see" and not as the individual may have awakened in them as to their abilities. This Jeremiah speaking for the first but not the last time. We are through. [See 900-428 on 3/8/29.]

(* Author's note: The "machine" referred to, I believe, is the [4666] Motor; see series of readings under 4665 on experiments with a perpetual motion machine which Messrs. [900] and [195] were financing with the inventor. Subsequent to 254-48 see further information on the machine in 195-57, 195-59 and 195-69.)

Edgar Evans Cayce poses here with his buddy of many years, Jack Sawyer, on one of the very few paved roads at that time in the Virginia Beach area. I can identify with the age, too, and those knickers the boys are wearing, something I'll bet they didn't really like either. Ecken was soon to enter Oceana High School.

(Above right) Mildred Davis, Gladys' cousin, joined the staff (late 1929) at a time when the hospital was thriving and the Association was growing. She stayed on to help after the hospital closed, then to become the Association secretary. The two young ladies are posed near the rear (south) entrance, where today a large magnolia tree stands.

(Above and right) The Squire stands in reverence to the memory of Carrie Elizabeth Cayce, to whom this fountain was being dedicated and who passed on in October 1926, just three years before. Directly to the left of the Squire's hat you can make out a trolley car waiting booth. The trolley or streetcar line ran from about 7th Street all the way into Norfolk, all of twenty miles, but was discontinued before World War II. Now in its place is a frontage road running close to the main arterial, Atlantic Avenue.

April 15, 1930

SPIRITUALISTIC RESEARCH AIM OF NEW ATLANTIC UNIVERSITY

PROPOSED VIRGINIA BEACH INSTITUTION INSPIRED BY WORK OF PSYCHIC HEALER, MORTON H. BLUMENTHAL, CHAIRMAN, REVEALS

(*New York Bureau of The Sun*)

New York, April 15—The proposed Atlantic University at Virginia Beach, Va., is being backed by a group who are deeply interested in psychic research and spiritualism, and it will be the only university in this or any other country to undertake psychic work, it was revealed today.

The university will be headed by Dr. William Moseley Brown, who resigned as professor of psychology at Washington and Lee University to run in the last Virginia Gubernatorial election with the backing of Bishop James Cannon, Jr., Republicans and the State's anti-Smith faction of Democrats. In this race he was decisively defeated.

Inspired by Psychic Healer

Dr. Brown in his announcement of the aims and ideals of the university a day or so ago listed a full course of the liberal arts and sciences and relegated psychic research to a footnote. However, Morton H. Blumenthal, whose brokerage offices are at 71 Broadway, New York City, and who is chairman of the board of trustees, said today the idea for the inception of Atlantic University really had sprung out of the work of Edgar Cayce, a psychic healer.

Mr. Cayce runs the Cayce Hospital for Research and Enlightenment at Virginia Beach and diagnoses patients who may be hundreds of miles away and whom he has never seen. According to Mr. Blumenthal, Mr. Cayce does this through his "subjective mind."

Boards Almost Identical

Back of the Cayce Hospital for Research and Enlightenment is a board which almost exactly duplicates the board that will run the new Atlantic University.

Thus, Mr. Bumenthal, his brother, Edwin D. Blumenthal, also of 71 Broadway, and a member of the Stock Exchange; David E. Kahn, of this city, a furniture manufacturer; Thomas B. Brown, of Dayton, Ohio, an engineer, and Franklin F. Bradley, of Chicago, a paint and varnish manufacturer, will finance and control Atlantic University as they do now the Association of National Investigators—the name of the organization behind the hospital.

To Study Mediumistic Work

Morton H. Blumenthal occupies the key position, however, inasmuch as he is chairman of the board of the university and president of the investigators' group. There also is another of the family connected with the investigators—Adeline Levy Blumenthal.

Furthermore, it is planned to make the hospital where Mr. Cayce's patients are treated an integral part of the university. That is, the students will be given an opportunity to study his mediumistic work.

Spiritualist Is Considered

From other sources it was learned that an Englishman—William G. Hibbins, B.S.A., a spiritualist, is being considered for the post of psychic research professor. Mr. Hibbins tried unsuccessfully to have the University of Sheffield, to which he is attached, install a similar professorship. He has written a preface to Mr. Blumenthal's book entitled "Heaven on Earth" and published by the Association of National Investigators. The book has a brilliant purple cover.

Mr. Blumenthal consented to an interview today in his office that is a byword throughout the financial district. It is furnished in super-modernistic fashion, precisely like some of the salons on the liner Bremen—a symphony in rich browns. Modernistic lamps light the place and in one corner is an etherealized figure on a pedestal representing an ascending angel without wings.

The photographer must have said: "Everybody squint for the camera." The Cayce-Evans cousins, left to right: Newton (caught standing) and Lynn Augustus Evans in front of Edgar Evans Cayce sitting beside Grandmother Elizabeth E. Evans (Gertrude's mom), and behind Hugh Lynn (in his ice-cream suit) is Chives Evans, all captured on film at the 35th Street Cayce home.

I have been informed on numerous occasions that Gladys and the Cayces frequented the beach at every opportunity, and here she offers us proof. (Top left, from left) Gertrude's brother, Lynn Evans, next to Elizabeth ("Beth") Graves, some open beach space, Gladys Davis, and a rather disinterested Hugh Lynn Cayce. In the next scene (center left) the ladies made a switch, possibly to appease the cameraman. (Lower left) The caption reads: "Patient and Nurse at the beach." Actually, he is Louis Francis, a prize patient who is "buried" (right) while getting a "gold treatment in accordance with the Cayce readings." The man lying next to him is Samuel J. Benstock. Lena Francis, Louis' daughter, is the girl in the hat, while the girl in swimsuit in both pictures is none other than Bella ("Billy") Sidelman, David E. Kahn's secretary. Linden Shroyer's son, Donald, is the little boy below.

This psychic reading given by Edgar Cayce at his office, 115 West 35th Street, **254-53**
Virginia Beach, Va., this 3rd day of March, 1931, in accordance with request made by Edgar Cayce himself and those individuals present.

PRESENT

Edgar Cayce; Gertrude Cayce, Conductor; Gladys Davis, Steno.
Annie, Hugh Lynn and L. B. Cayce, Mildred Davis, Sarah Hesson,
Gray Salter, and Elsie Swindall.

READING

WORK

Time of Reading
11:20 A.M. *Eastern Standard Time.*

Mrs. C: *You will have before you Edgar Cayce, present in this room, and the phenomena that manifests itself through him. Also all those individuals closely associated and interested in the furtherance of the work, and the circumstances that surround these and the phenomena itself. You will answer the questions for those so vitally interested, present in this room, answering the questions to each individually, as they themselves have asked them.*

Mr. C: *Yes, we have the phenomena—active; the conditions and circumstances that surround same in the present—now; also those interested in the furtherance of same.*

As has been given, there is definite work for each that would be, or at-tempt to be, a living example of that they themselves find presented to them through the information that may be gained for each, for groups, for individuals, for classes, for masses.

As these that are gathered, then, go about to gain that insight from within self as how to proceed with the varied conditions as affect each, then there is given that that will be the common basis upon which an association, an organization—physically speaking—may be builded. Let thy yeas be yea, thy nays be nay, in the light of that as is chosen for the purpose to be accomplished through the distribution, administration, of the information that is received through each; forgetting self, and building in that chosen as the ideal; not idea of, but an ideal!

First, in the beginning, then, those about the information, who have labored with or for—let them determine within theirselves whether they be willing to drink of the cup necessary; for, as is given, "Are ye able to drink of the cup I drink of?" to give this place or that place, or to sit on the right hand or the left is given by the Giver of all good and perfect gifts, according to the use of those talents, those abilities, each are given, or have builded by their associations with that as is held manifestedly in the heart and soul of each.

Then, when those here gathered have determined whether they are able, or are willing (for the strength is of the Giver), then call together such as have intimated or felt they would, in any manner, like to be associated with the undertaking.

In this place—here—Virginia Beach—as has been oft given—may the phenomena, the work, the distribution, the ministration to others, be better ex-

conditions as surround the various individuals who have been, who have labored together, who have labored once one against *another, those who have half-heartedly, those who have whole-purposefully—these offer an environmental condition, through the vibrations of the elements, that make for that which may become an exemplary manifestation of the light of the world, or may become the laughingstock of the world. For, as has been given, there are those forces innate in man, who is both God and the devil, that which put* into action *becomes the manifestation of* one *or the other of those* elementals *in the earth's forces.*

Then, call for such a gathering. Then choose from such as whole-heartedly are in accord with the findings that may have been, or may be given through the channels. Call such as those of local interest, those of the medium interest, those in the various spheres and walks of life. Then, from the meeting of such group choose that insignia, or name, or entitlement, under which the work will be physically manifested. Then ask if ye would receive, for as lots are cast for the choosing of the name, the choosing of a representative or manager—that is to be not *one of the governing board, but as one of the ones that represent, even as does the body through whom the information may come—and who also should* not—*should not—be a member of such governing board, but the source from which all questions, whether the choosing of a cook, or a physician, or a lawyer, be chosen. Not by the individual, but by all forces as would be in accord to make a oneness of purpose. Ready for questions.*

Q-1. Please suggest a name for the new organization.

A-1. It's just been given as to how it should be chosen! Why change it now? Why name it now? There are many minds to be considered, for such individuals locally—as those who manifest any show of interest—must, should, be chosen or asked to let them seek, and then ask to be a portion of such—and as they are chosen, or as they choose to stand on this side or that side, enroll same—see? Then, with a Board of at least twenty to twenty-five then a representative in whatever district there may be an interest shown shall be appointed to be the active force, that is a member of the governing board—but all questions shall be discussed with the manager—then presented, and not trouble the mind of the one through whom information comes with details, until they are asked for.

Q-2. In selecting an individual as a leader or manager, do you mean the selection of a business manager or a leader? That is, should the business manager also be the leader of the new organization?

A-2. Certainly not! The leader will always be that one through whom the information comes, whether Edgar Cayce or others that may be chosen to carry on—as Paul will enter in—with the work. [Paul Kaufman, who later became Chm. of Board?] [See 311-6, A-7] *In the choosing, then, it is the manager—who must not be a member of the governing board!* **[GD's note: A. C. Preston was later chosen by the Board as the first A.R.E. Manager.]**

Q-3. First questions, of Annie Cayce—Would it be well for me to take a house and have former patients come in and continue their treatments as they have expressed a wish to do?

A-3. It would be well! Take one sufficiently large to care for those that would come, and that would pay for the overhead and upkeep of same, having physician to visit and not live with, at, or even near—for these may be chosen from the many various fields, but maintain a registered—local registered nurse at all times as a portion of the work, that the good may not be evil spoken of by any. Enter into such an agreement with those that would aid in such a capacity, as a portion

142

of what—let same be a cooperative *basis, and as there are gradually added those* **254-53** *various things that may be applied, this will be the nucleus from which an institution* may *be raised.*

Seek from those that are gathered, when—either in person or by representative—those funds necessary for the maintaining of such a place, irrespective of anything that may be had from the income of those that are visitors. Then, when the group association, or *whatnot, is formed—this becomes a portion of the work. Don't be too hasty, but begin with* this *portion at once!*

Call together such as these, in less—within the next two weeks—setting a time. These may be local, these may be afar, these may be by wire, letter, or whatnot—see?

Scattergood, Taylor, Barnes, Wynne, Barrett, McChesney, Kahn, Levy, Taylor, and all those *who have intimated as those of Wyrick, Berger, Crews, and many others. Don't neglect* any!

Then, at such a meeting—such a meeting—this is a pre-organization, see? get sufficient to meet the needs of the hour. Hammerling should not be neglected; neither should those of Stern, nor any *of the various groups.* Again we *have come to that point wherein, as has been given aforetime, the leading force will be of the* house *of Israel, yet the* maintaining *power will be of the heathen.*

Q-4. Would I get full cooperation in this work?

A-4. If it's given, you will get it!

Q-5. Question by Sarah Hesson—What steps should be taken—first to begin reorganization?

A-5. As has been given.

Q-6. Question by L. B. Cayce—Will it be best for Edgar Cayce and for the work for it to be continued at Virginia Beach?

A-6. As has been given.

Q-7. If he should perfect another organization, should it be with a representative form of government?

A-7. As has been outlined, would be the better. Many minds make many *conditions. As has oft been given, the channels, the sources that* information *may be gained* from, *are unlimited. They will* not *defeat their purpose, provided* individuals *do not so project their* individual *personality as to* become *stumbling blocks. Take all thine troubles to Jesus! He cares!*

Q-8. Hugh Lynn Cayce—Direct Hugh Lynn Cayce as to how he can be of the greatest service at this time. What actual work can he do that will help the most?

A-8. The greatest help to each individual would be not *to argue with, but get down on the* knees *and pray with!*

Q-9. What actual work can he do that will help the most?

A-9. As each comes, and as each signify their willingness to serve, pray with. That's *actual work.*

Q-10. What steps should be taken by Edgar Cayce in seeing the Ass'n. legally dissolved? Should the claims of the life members be followed up and a settlement asked for?

A-10. (Interrupting before question was finished.) As has been given aforetime, as respecting the conditions that arose when differentiations and troublesome times arose, when that entity now known as Hugh Lynn Cayce banished from the face of men that priest [Edgar Cayce?] who had broken the vows that were leading a people to the light. The entity, then, has received again the light, through those physical *ministrations in the flesh in the present, in aiding individ-*

*uals to get a glimpse, through that of supplication to the source of all light, life,
and truth, that they themselves may be awakened to those potential powers that
lie within the breast of every individual to aid in ministering to the needs of
others. That, indeed a work! A labor worthy of him [Hugh Lynn Cayce?] that
called again to that body [Edgar Cayce], wrecked in the physical yet strong in
the power of counsel to the wayward, to the unseemly, to—though the ones
brought many of those forces that founded that faith in the Nazarene. Then as he
[Hugh Lynn Cayce?] led again those of his own household, and as he minis-
tered to those in the various fields of endeavor—indeed, then, be the minister, the
interpreter, to those who come to seek through these channels, these sources.
Help them to find their God, even as thou seest, thou knowest in thine self that
touch of His hand, thou knowest the care, thou knowest the tenderness, thou
knowest the way!*

We are through.

(Above) About 1948, the occupying tenant built the entrance driveway at the far left corner, while below you see it as the A.R.E. found it upon repurchase in 1956. These two scenes are utilized here *only* to show that Atlantic University had begun construction prior to Cayce Hospital's cessation of operations, as evidenced by foundations visible in both pictures, east of Atlantic Avenue, surrounded by surplus aircraft landing strip steel mats. (Below) The three-story house (upper extreme right) was rented by Edgar Cayce in July 1931, when he moved his family out of the 35th Street house, only to move again on March 1, 1932, to Lake Drive for a mere three months, and finally to Arctic Crescent, May 30, where he lived until his death on January 3, 1945.

On this 1971 aerial photograph by Aubrey Patterson Survey, Baltimore, Maryland, a broken line shows actual property lines for the Cayce Hospital and real estate on both sides of Atlantic Avenue, described on the previous page relative to Atlantic University's building plans. During the early '60s the old deteriorating concrete foundations were removed to make room for more automobile parking requirements of the U. S. Navy officers' beach club. The larger of the two observation towers was also removed at that time. A.R.E. was only able to get back the former property on this side of Atlantic Avenue, as outlined, mostly, in white broken lines.

146

A. C. Preston, the first manager of the newly formed Association for Research and Enlightenment. As you have just read in Reading 254-53 (which was given before the actual formation meeting in which A.R.E. superseded the earlier organization—Association of National Investigators), A.R.E. was officially incorporated in July 1931.

This portrait exemplifies the trend photographers adhered to during this period (1932), which was to allow too much of the subject's head to go out of focus. It's no great trick to accomplish, either, but it was fashionable. This photo was widely distributed as the one official public release photograph and was used until about 1938. (*Aufenger Studios, Norfolk, Virginia*)

COURT FREES CAYCE, REPUTED A 'PSYCHIC'

Magistrate Erwin Refuses to Interfere With "Beliefs of an Ecclesiastical Body."

WIFE AND AIDE DISCHARGED

Policewoman Tells How She Tested Powers of Virginia 'Diagnostician' In Hotel Suite Here.

Edgar Cayce, his wife, Gertrude, and his secretary, Gladys Davis, were discharged yesterday afternoon by Magistrate Erwin in West Side Court from a charge of "pretending to tell fortunes." Cayce is known at Virginia Beach, Va., where he has been a resident for several years, as a "psychic diagnostician."

Policewoman Bertha Conwell, who brought about the arrest of the three in their suite in the Victoria Hotel on Nov. 7, testified that she and another policewoman had visited him on that day, dictating to the secretary a list of questions she wished answered. They included advice on "a pain at the base of my brain and in my back" and "is this the right time to make certain investments I contemplate?" She said she was asked by Miss Davis to sign an application for membership in the Association for Research and Enlightenment, Inc., before the "reading" but that she refused, saying she might do so later if she became sufficiently interested.

The answers to the questions were among the papers in the case. The policewoman testified that they were given by Cayce as he lay on a bed with his eyes closed while his wife read the questions. She denied having signed any application for membership in the organization, but Mrs. Cayce and Miss Davis testified later that she did sign one, which had "disappeared" after the police removed a number of papers from the suite.

David E. Kahn, a furniture manufacturer of 44 West Seventy-seventh Street, testified that he was a director of the Association for Research and Enlightenment, Inc., and that it had been formed to investigate psychic phenomena, specifically the alleged gifts of Cayce, and it had about 2,000 members. He said all money collected went to the organization, which paid Cayce a salary.

"I make no claims whatever," said Cayce on the stand. "For thirty-one years I have been told I was a psychic. It first began as a child. I didn't know what it was. After it had gone on for years a company was formed to study my work."

In discharging the trio Magistrate Erwin said he found Cayce and his co-defendants not to be persons pretending to tell fortunes. "And to hold them guilty," he said, "would be to interfere with the beliefs of an incorporated ecclesiastical body."

Julien P. Proskauer, trustee of the Society of American Magicians, said that laws which the society would present to the January session of the State Legislature for adoption would "prevent the discharge in court of people pretending to have supernatural powers."

Once more, allow me to suggest reference to Gladys' book, *My Years with Edgar Cayce*, for a well-detailed rundown on what transpired following the closing of the Cayce Hospital, loss of the 35th Street house, and the situation prior to their finding this Lake Holly property (left). The Cayce family and Gladys laugh about it today, but admittedly it was far from amusing at the time. The new place was located at 308 Arctic Crescent, opposite where 14th Street enters Pacific Avenue, but a good two hundred feet from the intersection. Edgar Cayce is visible cultivating a section of his garden, a chore to many of us, yet a source of recreation and enjoyment to him. A few years later that garage would be moved to the other side of the house to make room for additions to the building, mainly office space for the growing A.R.E.

148

Despite being out-of-focus and generally in poor condition, I felt these two pictures were important contributions to our story. (Above) The Glad Helpers Prayer Group, photographed the same day, place, and by the same camera as the Norfolk Study Group No. 1 (shown below).

(Top left) Edgar Cayce sports a string of fish he caught in the St. Lawrence river while visiting the Buchanan family there. This has been quite widely used as a public relations photograph, especially with TV interview shows, based on the well-known fact that fishing was his favorite hobby. (Right) With his close friend, Mitch Hastings, and this trusty '33 Pontiac this picture shows Edgar Cayce holding the Pontiac at bay during a trip below the Mexican border, probably near Nogales, which is fairly close to Tucson, where he and Mitch were staying (76 Ranch, Bonita, Arizona—not far from Casa Grande where the new A.R.E. Clinic, Inc., is to be located).

(Left) Reminiscent of a slightly earlier age, the pose with hands in pockets, hat brims pulled down, one easily imagines the early 1920s (or perhaps some of you would more quickly relate to a Bonnie and Clyde movie). A bone-chilling morning atop the Empire State building in January 1934, finds (left to right) T. Mitchell Hastings, Jr., Hugh Lynn Cayce, Edgar Cayce, Gladys Davis, and Mrs. Carolyn (T.M.) Hastings.

It's traditional probably in every part of the United States, maybe throughout the world, to take visiting dignitaries, good friends, and family all about the area, showing them outstanding historical markers, maybe sharing a picnic outing with them, or even taking them to the best eating places. Edgar and Gertrude were no different. Here Gertrude's mother, Elizabeth Salter Evans, is receiving that kind of treatment, seeing Yorktown (a statue of Captain John Smith is the backdrop here), maybe Williamsburg and Jamestown later. This was Mrs. Evans' last visit to Virginia Beach, as she passed over in April 1934, certainly only a few months after this visit.

It must have been Gertrude's influence that got her own mother to remove her hat for this picture, but she holds onto it as though it did something for her morale. The date given both pictures was summer, 1933. Summer would account for Gertrude's attire, not so much as a lightweight sweater. To the stranger, summer in the Tidewater area gets as hot and sticky as any place you'll find in the U.S.A., including Florida.

ASSOCIATION FOR RESEARCH & ENLIGHTENMENT, INC.,
Virginia Beach, Virginia

March 29, 1933

Dear Members:

Today is the anniversary of the first reading, or
the first time information of a helpful nature came through this
channel.

It is about this work that I desire to talk with
each of you for a moment. Of course, many stages of development
and phases of the phenomena have been "cussed and discussed"
during the last thirty-three years.

There have been developments in the past year in all
phases of the Work (Study Group readings, Life Readings, and
Physical readings). Reports have been most gratifying; and I am
sure they would convince the most skeptical that the Work has
proven worth while in the experience of a great many.

The general economic condition, and more recently
the bank situation, has had an effect upon the public in connection with work of this nature as much as in other fields of a
more commercial nature.

This Work, we are persuaded, can be worth a great
deal more; if there will be a little more interest shown by the
members of the organization.

We are really in need of interest. More appointments
can be handled.

As an anniversary celebration, may I ask each one
of the membership to secure a new member or to make an appoint-
ment for a reading within the next ten days?

Soon we shall be making announcements for our
Annual Congress. We shall want as much interest and as large
a group present as possible. Will you do me the honor of writing
me about this?

We will send any data that you may desire, but what
we need is ACTION on the part of every member - NOW!

Thank you!

Ever the same,

Edgar Cayce

Edgar Cayce

EC:GD

The dedication ceremonies were so gratifying that Edgar just had to go out and catch the family dinner, which looks very much like a three-pound Virginia Beach spot (yes, that's really a type of fish, even though it sounds like a fish story). It might be called a Norfolk spot around Norfolk fishing areas.

This is about the only photograph that captures both Cayces laughing. Despite its poor condition, it inspired me to doctor it up to what you see here . . . so you could smile with them.

Can't you almost hear the photographer telling all of them to crowd-in a little closer together . . . "Hugh Lynn, put your arm around your mother and move over closer to her. We don't want any of the car to show between you." If the photographer did say that, then it almost got Gertrude Cayce squeezed out of sight.

(Above left) Edgar Evans Cayce graduated from high school and entered Duke University in 1935 to study electrical engineering. (Below left) Edgar Evans is pictured at the Louis B. Poss home in Alexandria, Virginia, the same year he graduated from Duke, 1939.

(Above right) Standing halfway across a wooden bridge spanning a narrow waterway of Lake Holly, which has since been filled in for "better" land development, Gladys Davis affectionately holds her nephew, Thomas Jefferson (TJ) Davis. (Below right) while Gertrude holds TJ, Carrie House patiently waits her turn.

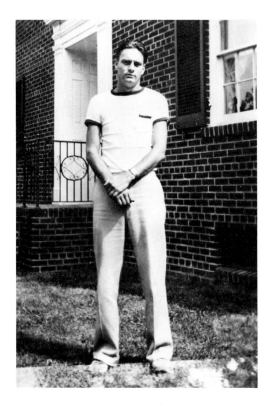

(Above) These Scarsdale, New York, Thanksgiving diners (1937) are, from left to right: hostess, Lucille Kahn; Gertrude and Edgar Cayce next; Mary Sugrue is partially hidden by her husband, Thomas, and a lighted candle; then David E. Kahn peeks around the lovely face of Gladys Davis, while Hugh Lynn Cayce almost hides the first born, S. David Kahn. Accompanying this photo, Lucille noted: ". . . the only party not showing, though present, was Dick." Hidden from camera at Lucille's left in his highchair was Richard Kahn, their youngest. The cameraman was the Kahn's servant, Job Patience, a follower of Father Divine. Indicating that this was right after he became ill, Thomas' cane was hung atop Lucille's chair back, mainly because his chair lacked hanger possibilities. (Right) Chapter 13 of *My Life with Edgar Cayce,* as told to Will Oursler by David E. Kahn, details Sugrue's illness and clarifies why Hugh Lynn stands behind Thomas in his wheelchair a few years later, during Cayce check-readings on Sugrue's progress with *There Is a River,* at Virginia Beach. (See photo, page 190.)

156

(Above left) As seen from the Cayce
floating dock (willow branches and
planter box visible at lower left corner),
the south rear view reveals brick construction of new office and vault additions, which David E. Kahn and Edgar
Cayce (above right) might have been discussing, or maybe the next construction
project, prior to dedicating the new space.

Harold J. Reilly received patients bearing
Cayce readings directed to him for treatment as early as 1931, long before the
physiotherapist ever heard of Edgar
Cayce. Jess Stearn devoted the entire
eighth chapter of his best seller, *Edgar
Cayce, the Sleeping Prophet,* to the fine
co-operative treatment and great skill
with which the famous physiotherapist
has aided Cayce patients in overcoming
their many and varied ailments.

157

Take a look at the dust jacket on the hardcover book, *My Years with Edgar Cayce,* by Mary Ellen Carter (the personal story Gladys Davis Turner told to Mrs. Carter). Thereon you will recognize an amazing similarity between that "doctored" reproduction and our trio (top left), a famous photo long before that book's publisher eliminated Gertrude from its perspective (bottom left). Posed outside the building's newly completed additions during dedication ceremonies in 1940, they were celebrating new office space and a new vault in which to store the many Cayce readings, and related correspondence.

(Left) Cayce brothers, Edgar Evans and Hugh Lynn, seem to be quite relaxed for this formal pose, which was taken at the same time as that of the family portrait on the facing page. (Center) Noah and Hannah Miller flank Esther Wynne (hiding in the shadow of her own hat and unconsciously wringing her hands) and Pat Bailey (having trouble with a stiff breeze trying to make off with her hat). This seems to be the only available picture of Noah Miller for this period. The Millers had many readings, especially Noah.

Most of the large group of celebrators are pictured here, among whom you may find familiar faces, including Edgar Cayce, if you look closely.

(Above) A Cayce family pose, an informal portrait, which was to appear many years later in Joseph Millard's book, *Edgar Cayce, Man of Miracles*. I feel that it must have been taken during the summer of 1940 prior to these dedication ceremonies. (Left) Hugh Lynn at left of Mrs. Louise B. Chisholm, who was to become a very active associate, and the recent bride, Sally Taylor Cayce (her bridegroom is the guy with the grin . . . as if you didn't know), who is still toying with her ceremonial rings—unconsciously, no doubt.

(Top left) Sally (holding onto her puppy), Gertrude, and Kathryn Cayce seem impatient with this picture-taking episode near the west side of A.R.E. Headquarters. (Below right) No identification is available for the upstaging dog, but that's Gertrude in black with close friend and staff worker, Mae Gimbert Verhoeven (later St. Clair).

(Above, center left) Mrs. Louise B. Chisholm and Gladys Davis became the best of friends. It was this friend who gave Gladys the piece of property next door to the Cayce's, where her home still exists today. (Bottom right) This was copied from a rather badly faded colored print that a number of individuals thought was such a good picture of the Cayces and Gladys Davis.

This portrait of Edgar Cayce (and those on pages 164 and 166) was the photographic work of Boice Studio, a Virginia Beach enterprise, which handled considerable amounts of A.R.E. requirements during this period, inasmuch as the Cayce photographic talents had been retired in favor of psychic phenomena.

Celebrated concert singer Lydia J. Schrader Gray was invited by Edgar Cayce to come to Virginia Beach and help run the A.R.E. Her keen interest stemmed from personal "life" readings Edgar Cayce gave for her, wherein it was indicated that she could better serve mankind by lecturing and teaching concepts from the Cayce readings. However, Lydia was unable to rearrange her life style and fulfill her promises to him until after the Cayces both passed over in 1945. Answering vast quantities of correspondence to help Gladys Davis was chore number one, but when the former hospital was bought back, between conference programs, Lydia took on housekeeping chores and the challenge of complete redecoration. Shriners' vast array of symbols covered walls, including life-size camels in natural desert surroundings from floor to ceiling in the living room (now the reception area). She financed it out of the program she devised for contributed trading stamps. Some received remuneration for numerology charts created for members, and this money also went toward redecoration.

Esther Wynne, one of the founders of A.R.E. Study Group activities and Study Group No. 1, and the one person most responsible for getting the *A Search for God* books published. Now, that's not saying there weren't many others involved in both areas, but she was the spark plug of the whole effort. If you check the *A Search for God, Readings Book I,* you will find the entire list, not only those involved in obtaining these important readings, but those twelve members of Study Group No. 1, along with background notes made by Gladys Davis. She was a great inspiration to today's International Study Group directors, the Sechrists.

163

(Previous page) This particular portrait of Edgar Cayce has that unmistakable air of an aristocrat, a certain elegance not found in others (okay, I'm entitled to my opinions, too). Dr. Harold J. Reilly (at left) was becoming a fairly frequent visitor, finding out what the Cayce readings were all about, and was incorporating more into his physiotherapy business in New York City. He was destined to utilize his research in a book he would publish in 1957, *Easy Does It,* but a more important book, *The Edgar Cayce Handbook for Health Through Drugless Therapy,* based on his forty-five years' experience and work with the Cayce readings, epitomized Dr. Reilly's ideals in 1975. (Below) All stimulated and most anxious, we find one Harmon H. Bro being encouraged by Edgar Cayce, probably toward quoting his readings accurately in the thesis about Edgar that would win Harmon his college degree (Ph.D.) from the University of Chicago, wherein his study depicted Edgar Cayce as a religious seer. Harmon Bro would become a formidable writer and lecturer in close association with A.R.E. functions.

This straight-forward Edgar Cayce pose has been the frontispiece throughout nineteen printings of Thomas Sugrue's great book, *There Is a River*.

The short period of time in which Edgar Cayce and Elsie Sechrist had to work together left no historical markers. Yet, it certainly inspired Elsie (along with the patience and understanding of husband, Bill) into enlightening ventures that developed Study Group growth wherever she lectured and to write a best-selling book based on Edgar Cayce's readings, much research, and experience, *Dreams—Your Magic Mirror* (this same photo appears on hardcover dust jacket rear panels). Mrs. Sechrist first met the Cayce family (which includes Gladys Davis) in 1943. (*Wilfred "Bill" Sechrist*)

Possibly the most famous, or most-often-seen Edgar Cayce photographic pose, is this "Thinker" portrait (title was attached prior to my arrival at the Beach). It is the same portrait used on all A.R.E. paperback *Edgar Cayce on . . .* series, such as *Edgar Cayce on Atlantis, Edgar Cayce on Reincarnation,* etc., besides being used extensively as the main publicity photo release to magazines, newspapers, TV, and other public relations means. Now non-existent, Knight Studio was the producer of this fine photographic portrait.

Taken from the front-door yard of the Catholic church, this scene gives you quite a different perspective of the Cayce home and A.R.E. Headquarters. It is also pretty good quality, considering that it is enlarged from a black-and-white negative of a color slide (35mm).

Although this is summer of '42, it relates in no way to a muchly awarded motion picture of the same title. Without their knowing it, Edgar Cayce and his four loving sisters gathered together for what was to be their last time, in Hopkinsville or any other place in this lifetime. Standing at left are Mary, Edgar, and Sarah, while Ola (left) and Annie sit below. One of the husbands probably shot the picture.

(Top left) Annie appears concerned for her famous brother, almost suspecting something, knowing full well how overworked he was and looking like it, too, yet she undoubtedly felt helpless to do anything about the situation.

(Below) Two familiar poses of the famed psychic; the one at left being similar to the left profile used later in *Edgar Cayce, Man of Miracles,* but I prefer this laughing one. The garden pose (right) is included just so you might identify Edgar Cayce with the flowers he loved so much and tenderly nurtured (he often talked to them while cultivating and tending their needs). Those are climbing roses pictured, but he had a special rapport with other flowers, too. Already, however, he had little or no time to spend with them, and when *There Is a River* came out a few months hence, they were destined to have no further contact, as sad as it seems.

This famous photograph of Edgar and Gertrude Cayce, taken from a 35mm color slide, bears a 1943 date, which was undoubtedly taken about the same time as the group picture of the family that was chosen to appear in Joseph Millard's book (hardcover), *Edgar Cayce, Man of Miracles.* This particular pose has been most often requested, probably because more individuals, especially newcomers to the A.R.E., have seen it in the Association's *Introductory Brochure* (about 450,000 have been published). Here, however, it has been reversed (deliberately) so that the elders are facing the 40-years-younger Cayce couple on the opposite page. This shows the famous psychic at the time he was giving many times more clairvoyant readings than his own readings condoned (they warned him he was overdoing). He was deeply concerned over the young men lost or missing in the war (World War II), out of literally hundreds of requests for readings from loved ones, who were more concerned, of course.

172

This charming photograph of the newlyweds is deliberately out of chronological order, if for no other reason than to show the culmination (previous page) of forty years of marital maturity and, here, the very beginning.

In order to gain nearly half an inch of picture hidden behind its framing, I removed Gertrude and Edgar Cayce's portrait (preceding page) from its original folder matting. I automatically turned it over and found this bearded gentleman staring back at me, but with no information about him any place. I must admit that I don't know why photographs were occasionally back-to-back in this manner, unless it was a scarcity of photographic printing paper, which is special quality.

"Meanwhile, back at the ranch," Thomas Sugrue had completed his story of Edgar Cayce manuscript and had submitted it to his publisher, who responded by publishing his masterpiece in December 1942. Thomas Sugrue had actually done preliminary outlining and much readings research during his earlier visits from 1927 through '31, before his journalistic tendencies involved him in newspaper writing and foreign assignments for such notable publications as the *American Magazine* (he briefly accounts for his coverage of the Cayces' court trial in New York in this book). The wheelchair-stricken author returned to the Cayce home in 1939, submitting his writing to the close scrutiny of Edgar Cayce's check readings until he was enthusiastically satisfied the material was ready for publication. He also points out that typing chores were accomplished by his patient wife, to indicate that no further burden was placed on A.R.E.

THERE IS A RIVER

The Story of Edgar Cayce

by

THOMAS SUGRUE

HOLT, RINEHART AND WINSTON
New York • Chicago • San Francisco

174

No other picture of Edgar Cayce projects the informality and personal appeal that this pose offers. Wilfred ("Bill") Sechrist captured this film classic almost immediately after these two first met. Never before published, Bill thought it most appropriate for this book.

A similar view of these fishing partners has appeared some 350,-000 times in the A.R.E.'s public relations piece called *Introductory Brochure*. It does not have Edgar Cayce's floating shade tree, nor the facts about it and his floating pier, however (both were his own invention). Both sank during a storm.

Despite the fact that no picture exists in the Edgar Cayce Foundation files that shows the Cayce floating shade tree doing its designed function, it was frequently utilized merely by simple manipulation of control ropes and anchored, thus shading the concentrating fishermen from the hot summer sun.

Although vegetable gardening was more work than the loving care of his flowers, Edgar Cayce became a fairly good city farmer. Although the readings suggested that everybody work the soil whenever possible, this was only one of many reasons for Edgar's gardening efforts. Relaxation and exercise probably had more to do with his motives than anything else. Besides, the whole family liked fresh vegetables.

Unfortunately, today Lake Holly is about half the size it was when this picture (above) was taken (1941), then only two-thirds the size the Cayces found it to be in 1925 upon their arrival. Anyway, where you see water here, today there exists a parking lot for the Catholic church. Even with this additional office space, trying to accommodate numerous notable researchers, handle greater reading demands, growing membership, larger lecture attendance, etc., the building would be sufficient, as shown below, for another six years before more space became imperative. About 1960, the old headquarters was converted into small apartments, wherein a few A.R.E. staff members lived, despite the fact that the place was *not* owned or operated by A.R.E. On September 12, 1976, the "landmark" was burned down by the Virginia Beach Fire Department on the orders of the Catholic church (its new owners of two years), on which location a childrens' playground was built.

177

Presumably, Edgar Cayce's steadier, more experienced hand tripped the camera shutter for this group picture, and managed to promote pleasant expressions on practically every face. This included most of those attending the 1943 A.R.E. Congress.

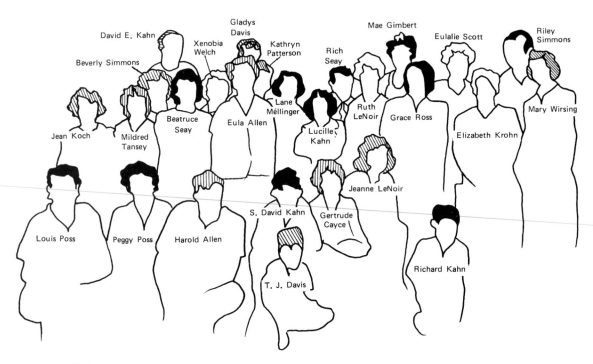

David E. Kahn
Gladys Davis
Mae Gimbert
Eulalie Scott
Riley Simmons
Xenobia Welch
Kathryn Patterson
Rich Seay
Beverly Simmons
Jean Koch
Mildred Tansey
Beatruce Seay
Eula Allen
Lane Mellinger
Lucille Kahn
Ruth LeNoir
Grace Ross
Elizabeth Krohn
Mary Wirsing
Jeanne LeNoir
Louis Poss
Peggy Poss
Harold Allen
S. David Kahn
Gertrude Cayce
Richard Kahn
T. J. Davis

The culprit who fuzzied-up this picture could quite possibly be one of those missing here but present in the one opposite. This almost duplicate pose was undoubtedly snapped to show Edgar Cayce, Elsie Sechrist, and Esther Wynne, who were absent from the other shot. These identification charts wouldn't have been possible without Gladys Davis Turner's fabulous memory and co-operation. Both poses have been enlarged from original 120 negatives.

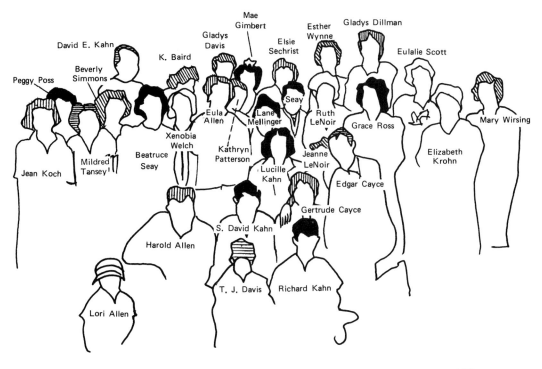

(Left) "Eddie and Muddie Cakie" were young TJ's (Thomas Jefferson Davis) learning-to-talk names he attached to the Cayces. A Davis family member caught this scene during a Cayce visit to Montgomery, much to TJ's obvious delight.

(Below) It was Annie Cayce who took over housekeeping duties at Cayce Hospital when Dr. House died and Carrie went back home. Edgar stoops into the picture behind his sister Annie, with sister Sarah and her husband, L. J. Hesson, beside and to her right (your left). All are posed near the street in front of the Arctic Crescent A.R.E. Headquarters and Cayce home, the Catholic church visible in left background.

(Left) "EC took picture," is part of the caption. Nobody (well, almost nobody) could have predicted that the print wouldn't keep too well, which accounts for it being slightly gray across the middle. The ladies, Gladys Davis and her good friend Viola Beck (Shaw) must have been most persuasive to get Edgar Cayce away from so much work. Perhaps that's why they didn't go any further away than right outside the office door. 1943.

(Below) This is "the office force, 1944." From far left, Gladys Davis, Mary Wirsing, Jean Fitch, Gertrude Cayce, Betty Corson, Willa Iron, and Mae Gimbert Verhoeven (Mae St. Clair), while June and Harmon Bro's smiling faces shine from behind the group.

(Above) Edgar Cayce with his friend of many years, W. L. Jones from Selma, a charter member of Edgar's famous *Sevenette* Sunday school class. Cayce Jones, W. L. Jones' son, was named for our hero and later became active in A.R.E.

(Above right) Edgar poses in his own back yard, close to his former favorite recreational implement—his fishing pier and willow shade tree, with which he was now an almost total stranger. Many hundreds of friends and visitors walked in this area, partaking of its great vibrations and possibly never realizing what made it so special. (Bottom left) David E. Kahn, Gertrude and Edgar Cayce, with Lucille Kahn, all posing in an early afternoon sun for a close friend or relative, but again in the Lake Holly yard. Kahn readings were numerous, dating back many years, and many others had benefited from them, as did they themselves. Gratitude was not lacking from either David or Lucille.

182

(Above) Despite having given up photography when he left Selma for Dayton, Edgar did not lose his love for photos themselves, as the walls of his office verified. You might recognize a picture here and there. That oval-framed portrait at the center rear of Edgar's desk is the same Christmas gift Gertrude had given him forty-four years before (I'm sure she still had the one he gave her, too). The 1944 calendar in the corner covers up an aura chart that has since been reproduced in the A.R.E. press booklet *Symbols and the Self*.

(Right) A non-fishing pair whose backs appear earlier in much warmer weather. It's quite possible that young TJ Davis has just arrived from school, unless I'm wrong and that's not a school book bag he has strapped to himself. Edgar Cayce was a strong influence on this boy's life.

(Left) From left: Harmon Bro, Gladys Davis, Kathryn Patterson, and Hugh Lynn Cayce, all with that expression of anticipation, perhaps wondering why it should take so long just to snap a picture (if more time was spent taking meaningful pictures . . . well, that's another story). (Below right) I don't recollect ever seeing another photo of just these two without at least Gertrude or some other individual included.

(Above) Harold J. Reilly was becoming a frequent visitor at A.R.E. Headquarters (during the Depression and war years, every two years could be qualified as frequent). He was working toward the day when there would be an A.R.E. Therapy Department.

A somewhat historic occasion! The first grandson of Gertrude and Edgar Cayce, begat for them by number one son; Hugh Lynn and co-operative wife Sally produced Charles Thomas Cayce, who wins with his smile.

Possibly secondary in historical values here, Hugh Lynn, in U. S. Army uniform—the picture of a happy father, who had already joined up and was about to fulfill the Army's request for his services in the European war zone, where his brother, Edgar Evans, was already seeing action. (Left) The way Sally holds her son confirms a thought that he must have been very energetic, probably a truly "bouncing baby boy." Do you suppose that Gertrude could have been wondering if this would be the last time she would be with *her* son? Her detached or far-away expression leads one to speculate. She would have been right.

In *There Is a River,* Thomas Sugrue's eloquence and elaboration covered the growth and progress of the Cayce family in great detail, including how the boys felt toward various titles attached to their psychic father, as well as Gertrude's viewpoint. In it you will find more about the boys. Here they have married lovely young women (Below: Sally —front left—sits in front of her husband, Hugh Lynn—they married one year before Edgar Evans and Kathryn—front right), and were facing overseas military obligations, and did not even suspect that this might be their last photograph with their parents—nor did Edgar and Gertrude.

As both Edgar Evans and Hugh Lynn quickly admit, their mother, Gertrude Cayce, readily shared with them and Edgar, not only the good with the bad, but her honest, forthright, and often blunt viewpoints of almost any situation in which her family was involved. No only was she Edgar's "helpmate" and closest friend, she kept him in balance (often with Gladys Davis' moral support), while guiding him through her role of "Readings Conductor." Another unheralded great woman behind a great and famous man.

There Is a River stimulated an immediate interest far beyond the Cayces' and A.R.E.'s wildest dreams, yet created a whole new agonizing situation over and above existing problems, which, with Hugh Lynn away in the Army, added new strains to Gertrude's already overburdened talents. Normal postman deliveries became obsolete, and Gertrude had to pick up mail in the family car. Besides a dozen readings daily, Edgar pitched in reading and dictating answers to literally scores of letters, which practically eliminated his recuperative naps between readings sessions and further taxed his already rundown physical system. This picture of Gertrude and Edgar, probably taken during the '44 Congress, reveals how tired-to-the-bone both had become at this period. Two months later Edgar collapsed and had to go away to rest. He returned home for Thanksgiving and died on January 3, 1945.

Mourning will never bring back the dead, and it is safe to assume that Edgar and Gertrude Cayce would have wished for things to continue in a better-than-normal manner, but not overlooking directions given through him in the readings that would serve as guidelines, even as spiritual light, if the ideals and purposes were right. The above group, A.R.E. Congress program registrants, were all quite aware of the circumstances and set about doing something constructive. One in particular, Gina Cerminara, authored two outstanding books that are still in print today (*Many Mansions* and *The World Within*).

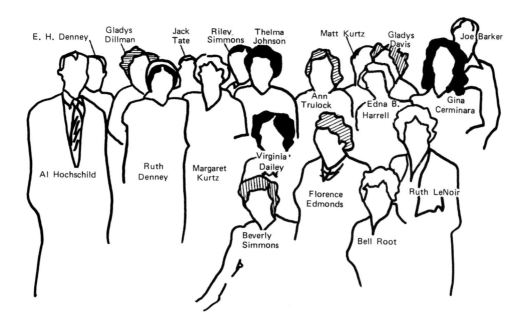

(Left to right) Tiny Helen Honeck beside Lydia J. Schrader Gray with our own Gladys Davis giggling along with Gina Cerminara.

(Left) Hugh Lynn partially hides Cayce Jones, while Eric Nilson glances at the cameraman, and Thomas Sugrue is pensive, possibly thinking of his next book, or the journal, *The New Tomorrow*.

These three pictures reveal one major factor. A.R.E. was carrying out its set ideals and purposes despite the great loss of its beloved leaders, Gertrude and Edgar Cayce.

(Below) Looks like a discussion centered around Thomas Sugrue, who was back revising *There Is a River*, with Hugh Lynn Cayce (behind Sugrue) possibly awaiting something printworthy for the *Membership Bulletin*.

Probably the same day, or weekend, as the preceding photo (the clothing worn is the same), possibly right after a lecture by almost anyone facing the camera: Thomas Sugrue, Eula Allen (back to tree, standing), Lydia J. Schrader Gray (seated in front of Hugh Lynn Cayce, who might have talked). The other three women sporting sunglasses are Beverly Simmons, Peg Poss, and Jane Williams. Young men's heads, Eric Nilson (nearest Sugrue) and Cayce Jones, while Hannah Miller's back is to us.

(Left to right) Annie C. Davis (Gladys' mother), Florence Edmonds, Gladys Davis, Malcolm Allen, Eula Allen, Dorothy Morrisette, Hannah Miller. For several years volunteers, known around A.R.E. as the "Wednesday Shift," met on that day to mail out the weekly *Diary Letter to the Members from the Secretary,* and Dorothy, Gladys, and Annie were invited to pose with the group for this picture in April 1947.

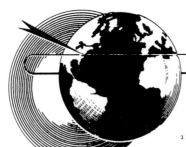

May 14, 1947

The house is overflowing today with a mixture of out of town visitors and our Norfolk Wednesday Shift. The regular staff always looks forward to Wednesdays, because Hannah Miller usually brings some of her wonderful home-made bread, and Eula Allen mixes a big green salad—now and then bringing one of her delicious home-made cakes. So, what with a contribution here and there of some delicacy, we usually have a grand free-for-all picnic.

VISITORS Mr. and Mrs. Myron Mohler of Baltimore, Md., are still with us. Others visiting Association Headquarters this week include: Mrs. Clara Adams of New York City; Mrs. Bertha D. Holley and daughter, Miss Marcia Holley, of Harrison, N.Y.

NEW YORK MEMBERS and friends will want to be sure to attend *THOMAS SUGRUE'S* last lecture of the season, on Monday, May 26th, 8:30 P.M., at Freedom House, 20 W. 40th St. His subject will be:

THE SPIRITUAL PATTERN OF AMERICA. The enclosed announcement should be mailed immediately to some friend whom you feel is interested.

Hugh Lynn Cayce will be present at the meeting. Definite *plans will be announced* for the Fall lecture program and group activity in the New York area.

WASHINGTON, D.C. Study Group is also sponsoring a lecture on May 26th, 8:00 P.M., at the Universalist Church, 16 & S Sts.

Mrs. Lydia J. Schrader Gray will be the speaker. Her subject: *EDGAR CAYCE AS I KNEW HIM.*

"THE CONGRESS THIS YEAR," (June 23–28) writes Harmon Bro, "coincides with a community-wide Vacation Bible School of which I have charge. That and the new baby seem to have me roped. But I am not closing any mental doors. . . .

"I will wire you when the baby arrives. If any of you feel like giving a life-reading for it, we will be happy to have it. We are holding off the names to see if we can guess a fitting one when the youngster arrives. Any suggestions?"

Rev. Joseph B. Clower, Jr., of Morganton, N.C., now spending a few days in Virginia Beach, says that he will be unable to attend our Congress this year because these dates happen to be the dates for the Young People's Conference of the Presbytery, and he is on the staff of the Conference.

Rev. Frank Carter Hawkins (Blackstone, Va.) writes from St. Louis, Mo., where he is in attendance upon the Southern Baptist Convention:

"My son and I wish to attend your Congress. . . .

"You will be happy to learn that the Southern Baptist Convention continues to spawn an increasing number of Truth seekers."

WHAT DO THE CAYCE READINGS OFFER THE AVERAGE CHURCH MEMBER?

This is the subject of the first lecture of the Congress. It was the question Mr. Cayce asked himself constantly through the years. Harmon Bro, according to his recent letter, is also seeking the answer to it. He says, in part:

"I am working on my doctorate and carrying a full-time church in the little town of Lanark, next to Mt. Carroll, Ill. . . .

"To complete an outline for a thesis I have just worked out the enclosed statement with the President of the University of Chicago. I want you to glance over it and put it into my file."

As Hugh Lynn says, we'd like to hang it on the wall instead of putting it in the files! Side by side, this proposal and Harmon's life reading make extremely interesting reading. We can't resist the urge to quote briefly from it:

"*MYSTICISM* is the broad area in which I have chosen to work, because I am thinking and acting along such lines in my own pastoral activity. I need the help which such a study can give me. . . .

"*A study of the work of Edgar Cayce,* specifically, I suggested for my thesis area . . .

"*My own interest in the Christian ministry* is directly related to the experience of observing and studying this man. In proposing him for thesis work I am simply operating on the old principle of 'a fellow does the best job on something he's interested in'. . . .

"I would like to bring the thesis to a close with a statement of what seems to me

"*THE SIGNIFICANCE OF THE WORK OF ONE MAN SUCH AS THIS . . .*

"Is there a basic pattern to 'mystical' experiences under similar conditions, or are these more subjective and individual? . . .

"What of claims for 'extra-sensory perception' in and out of religion? How [to] classify and analyze these, including Cayce's experiences? . . .

"What is the relation between extra-sensory gifts and mysticism? Which gives rise to which? Or are they usually unrelated? . . .

"What is the possible future in American Protestantism for various types of mysticism, both of thought and practice? What elements in the thought of Edgar Cayce make it easily absorbed into Protestant thought; what elements make it difficult?

"Etc. . . ."

Love and bye now,
GD.

An example of the *Diary Letter,* dated May 14, 1947.

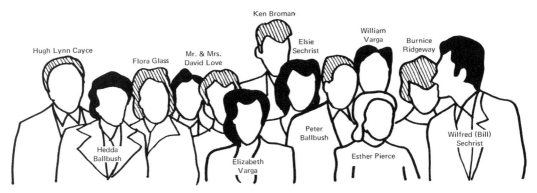

Hugh Lynn Cayce   Flora Glass   Mr. & Mrs. David Love   Ken Broman   Elsie Sechrist   William Varga   Burnice Ridgeway

Hedda Ballbush   Elizabeth Varga   Peter Ballbush   Esther Pierce   Wilfred (Bill) Sechrist

Gertrude and Edgar Cayce expected the "work" to continue without them and long after they were gone, as it did and is doing. These particular Study Group and Lecture/Conference organizers (more specifically, Sechrists) had been actively engaged in the "work" for the Association before the premature passing of the beloved Cayce pair. Earlier pictures of most of them were unavailable. I show this fine picture to fill that vacancy and to emphasize their great capabilities and the Study Group growth they stimulated on the Pacific Coast (mainly Los Angeles at this time). The year was 1948 and they were on the roof of a local radio station where some interview programming had been arranged. Of course, there were many others involved in activities such as this, but you are looking at the real promoters.

194

On the preceding page, I may have led you to believe there were large numbers of "A Search for God" Study Groups just on the Pacific Coast, when there actually were only nineteen organized Study Groups across the country meeting regularly. However, to the A.R.E. and the hard-working organizers, nineteen was then like the nearly two thousand affiliated Study Groups are to them today. Today these A.R.E. Study Groups work with *A Search for God* material (two hardcover textbooks and two looseleaf work books of verbatim Cayce readings, plus a guidance handbook).

Most of those original members of Study Group Number One, that you saw earlier, worked with the Cayce readings for eleven years, as the readings directed them to do, before the *A Search for God* books were ready. Book I was published in 1942 (before *There Is a River* came out), and Book II came along in 1950. Both are pretty much as they were then, with only minor revisions being necessary.

This *A Search for God* Study Group was also a research group, meeting here in Virginia Beach during 1950, as one of those very important nineteen groups. You may have recognized some of the group members. Left to right, Marjorie Bonney, Harmon Bro, Ruth Gimbert, Louie I. Davis, Gladys Davis, and Hugh Lynn Cayce. This took place in A.R.E. Headquarters at Lake Holly.

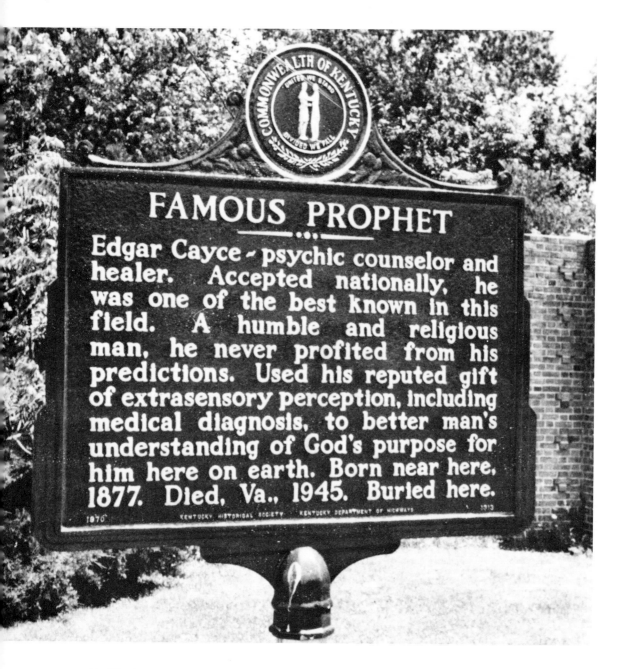

FAMOUS PROPHET

Edgar Cayce - psychic counselor and healer. Accepted nationally, he was one of the best known in this field. A humble and religious man, he never profited from his predictions. Used his reputed gift of extrasensory perception, including medical diagnosis, to better man's understanding of God's purpose for him here on earth. Born near here, 1877. Died, Va., 1945. Buried here.

1870   KENTUCKY HISTORICAL SOCIETY · KENTUCKY DEPARTMENT OF HIGHWAYS   1913

In Hopkinsville, Kentucky, this historical marker doesn't memorialize the physical man as much as it does what he tried to bring to the world; the God-given heritage of *life* that seeking minds will continue to find physically rewarding, mentally stimulating, and spiritually fulfilling, for at least another hundred years.

KENTUCKY, NEW ERA.

Hopkinsville, Ky., July 2, 1974

From Christian [County]

NATIVE SONS, DAUGHTERS MARK HISTORY OF NATION

by Mary D. Ferguson,

NEW ERA *Staff Writer·*

From the native sons and daughters of Christian County the state and the nation has gained congressmen, leaders in medicine, religious leaders, pioneer professional women, writers, noted physicians, the only president of the Confederate States of America and perhaps the most respected clairvoyant the world has ever known.

Edgar Cayce, clairvoyant, who has gained in popularity and respect far more during the days since his death than when he lived, was born in Christian County in 1877.

The Beverly community was the home of the Cayce family when the child who was to become a world famous psychic was born.

In December 1893, he and his family moved to Hopkinsville where as a young man he became a photographer.

He developed a God-given gift of extrasensory perception including an ability to give medical diagnosis.

A humble and religious man, Cayce never profited financially from his gift. He founded the Association for Research and Enlightenment at Virginia Beach, Va., where he died in 1945.

Cayce is buried near the chapel in Riverside Cemetery here.

With visitor numbers already doubled at the new A.R.E. Library/Conference Center, 2,000 visitors a month* viewed this old library setting. Occupying 384 three-ring, 2½-inch thick looseleaf binders, I photographed the contained Edgar Cayce readings just prior to their move into new quarters. As you can readily see, these volumes occupied two separate bookcases directly opposite each other, with researchers' table and chairs in between them (which were moved from the scene to allow a less-cluttered view). They were so arranged for many years. When you consider this vast source of psychic material, the thousands of pages, millions and millions of words, it is also necessary to realize there is pertinent correspondence related directly to most of these readings, literally thousands of items that make up the memorabilia connected with the life and work of Edgar Cayce. These historical records are being prepared in archival form by the Edgar Cayce Foundation staff, so they will be available for researchers in all areas pertaining to Edgar Cayce and the readings.

* Based on yearly averages, peak summer visitations often quadruple winter figures, periods of less A.R.E. activity and Virginia Beach resort attraction.

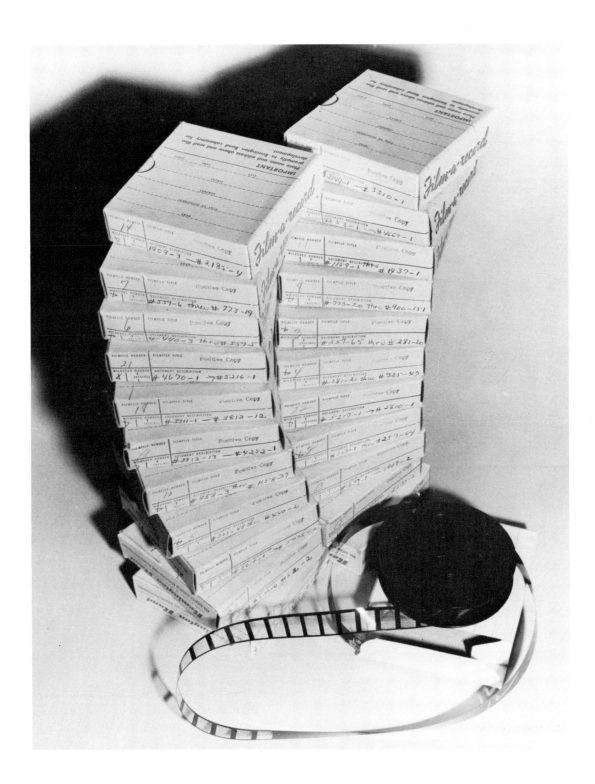

Can you visualize this? Three teetering stacks of typewritten paper (Xerographic copy on both sides), each a few inches taller than a six-foot man, were microfilmed into something over 55,200 images on these twenty-three 100-foot 16mm reels, of which there are three sets stored in as many different security places (one set in the U. S. Library of Congress under copyright). A negative set supplies reprints of original Edgar Cayce readings when a deteriorated copy requires replacement.

One of at least three Norman Mingo renderings—this was done from the "Thinker" photo of Edgar Cayce shown earlier—graced a fine article by Edgar Evans Cayce as told to Vaughn Shelton, "Miracles Were My Father's Business" which appeared in *Fate* magazine. The article was reproduced and distributed as free literature by A.R.E.

These two artist modifications of the Edgar Cayce portrait done by Boice Studio (Virginia Beach) that appeared as the frontispiece in Thomas Sugrue's *There Is a River* received little encouragement, acclaim, or enthusiasm at A.R.E., where they originated with former A.R.E. press layout artist David Wilson, who did see them used quite extensively on lecture program announcements throughout many parts of the U.S.A.

The A.R.E. produced this reprint from *The Commonwealth* (August, 1965), a Virginia Chamber of Commerce publication, and distributed it as a public relations item (free literature) over a period of eight years. The A.R.E. press altered the magazine layout to emphasize the Edgar Cayce name and illustration more proportionate to a give-away piece than the magazine article offered.

Dreaming of the future, probing the mass consciousness of the universe, leaping great voids of space and time: such were the fantastic pursuits of

EDGAR CAYCE

Astonishing psychic of Virginia Beach

By **LYTLE W. ROBINSON**

A FAMOUS ENGLISH scientist and author once said, "I am too much of a skeptic to deny the possibility of anything." Thousands of skeptics—among them psychologists, physicians, clergymen, businessmen, college students—have gone to Virginia Beach to see the nation's strangest collection of documents. And they leave shaking their heads in wonder.

Locked in a fireproof vault at the headquarters of The Edgar Cayce Foundation is a collection of psychic records unlike any other in the world. They are the 15,000 clairvoyant discourses of one man—all given while he was in a state of self-hypnosis.

Edgar Cayce (pronounced *Casey*), a modest, unassuming farm boy, photographer, and Sunday school teacher, was high in ESP—extra-sensory perception. He had the extraordinary gift of putting himself to sleep at will and discussing in an authoritative manner hundreds of subjects far beyond the range of his normal knowledge. He correctly predicted the sex of unborn infants, described personalities he didn't know, solved the "perfect" crime while 1,000 miles removed from the scene, successfully diagnosed and prescribed treatments for patients he never saw. Twice a day in broad

Over the past seventy years, literally hundreds of photographs of Edgar Cayce were not only used "straight," but commercial artists altered, "doctored," or characterized them in many and varied ways (some, I feel, were even "butchered" under the excuse that they meant well), all to draw immediate attention. You will see some of the most popular graphic arts renderings on these pages, more or less in the order of their importance and according to how often they were utilized.

The profile rendering (right) by Norman Mingo—which was drawn from a popular photograph you saw earlier—has undoubtedly appeared in print more often than all the others combined.

THE EDGAR CAYCE

PHOTOGRAPHIC SALON

Herein one may find satisfaction, as I have, in the fact that these fine photographic achievements possess a quality seldom found in modern, or contemporary works, which, to me, indicates some success for Cayce's formula based on simplicity.

Considering that this man was working under adverse conditions and was attempting to create unique photographic products of pleasing quality for each individual customer, while handicapped with being sought after, researched, investigated, ridiculed, and often used unscrupulously by selfish enterprisers, I must classify his efforts as extraordinary.

There was technological adversity too. The era of flashbulbs came about after Edgar Cayce had Gertrude sell his Selma photographic business and tools of trade to join him in Dayton. Photographic flash powder was famously inconsistent, unreliable, and dangerous, as were early flashbulbs (allow me to show my burn scars from exploding flashbulbs).

Today's "available light" snapshooter boasting mastery of this "new" field of photography knows little of its history. Edgar Cayce had it far better than earlier pioneers of the profession, yet he was trapped with studio requirements built around daylight illumination supplied best through large skylights and controlling pulleyed shades, not unlike many artist and sculptor studios.

With today's automatic cameras and electronic exposure computation, even the sophisticated hand-held light meters that came about after the Cayce period are becoming obsolete in favor of through-the-lens (TLS) built-in computors (still restricted to miniature equipment at this time). Consider this automation in relation to film speeds (emulsion exposure index, if you wish) ranging from a slow 25 to 500 in most common use today, against the staggering, unbelievable film speeds of 2 to 10 of that time (glass or celluloid based emulsions were most common, with the word "film" yet to be applied, and celluloid bringing along a fire hazard you wouldn't believe).

The baby (now a grown woman) in this madonnalike portrait of mother and daughter contributed this Edgar Cayce photograph to our cause and the archives, through Gladys Davis Turner's tour of the Deep South and visit to Selma in 1972. Needless to say, the pose and photography are unique and another fine example of this craftsman's mastery of his trade. Some restoration and darkroom manipulation was necessary in order to achieve these near-original results.

The Edgar Cayce Foundation/The Association for Research and Enlightenment Inc., Virginia Beach, Virginia

For some time I have been meaning to write to you to tell you that my mother knew Edgar Cayce in Selma, Alabama. She was teaching school there (this would have been before 1920). He was a photographer there and taught her Sunday school class. She has a number of photographs he took of her. I have one of them imprinted in the lower right corner "Cayce Art Co." I think that she never had a reading. If having prints of these photographs would be of any help to you, I imagine she would be delighted to have some made and send them to you. She remembers him as a very good man as well as amazingly clairvoyant. Considering the equipment of that time, I also think he was an exceptionally fine portrait photographer.

Sincerely,

(Mrs.) Patricia Freeman

This portrait was made in Hopkinsville in early 1911. Carrie Major Cayce is wearing a very dark fur collar here, which accounts for the appearance of the head and body separation, at least, where the fur reflects no light at all.

The expressions alone in this intimate Cayce portrait of his wife and youngest son suggest that he might have had some difficulty bringing seriousness to this setting, but here he did manage to capture something unique. Gertrude Cayce, as son Edgar Evans will verify, was not only a beautiful woman in many ways, but was a most loving, attentive, and guiding element of remarkable stature to him, revealed somewhat by his own expression here.

It is doubtful that this was a commercial photo. Your compiler's opinion is that Hugh Lynn Cayce's mother simply wanted memorable portraiture of their unique offspring. I can't say much in favor of kids' clothing styles, especially for boys of that period. Heck no, I like the cap and sweater! There's something even more interesting about that chair, which is not too unlike some current import items.

For the family and relatives, besides an opportunity, possibly, for practicing new darkroom printing techniques. Again, Hugh Lynn is beginning to lose his baby fat, facial chubbiness, etc. There undoubtedly were hundreds of children's portraits that received similar technique treatment, for which this serves as a prime example.

Here big brother reveals genuine affection for his little baby brother. Again it's Hugh Lynn and Edgar Evans Cayce.

Chronology has little importance in this special salon section of this book, but it is true (and obvious) that this is an earlier pose of the Cayce brothers than the preceding one. However, I wanted this set aside all by itself. To me, their individual expressions are absolutely priceless! I hope that Edgar Cayce caught them deliberately just for that value alone. It appears to be Hugh Lynn's first venture into holding very fragile new babies, and I wonder if baby is not showing his anticipation of his brother's uncertainty.

Gertrude Cayce's twin sister is pictured nowhere else in this entire book because this is the only existing photograph of her—them—together. (No mystery, really. Actually most photographers will at some time or other do a bit of photographic experimenting. Darkroom manipulation and, as in this instance, multiple exposed films of a single object—his favorite model. Utilization of a deep black background, precise lighting, and a patiently interested model, plus great skill—the alternative to which is lots of costly practice. The result is this near-perfect photograph worthy of any salon.) Sorry, a twin she's not, but a convincing double exposure of herself she is.

(Above) By now, it would be of little surprise to anyone that the two Cayce boys were frequently photographed merely from family interest and for record, just as is common practice in millions of families today (true, it wasn't awfully commonplace then). Mellin's Food for the Baby, one of many canned goods by this company, became a household word at the Cayces' following widespread success of this Cayce photo-ad.

(Right) From a miniature, this portrait of mother and son (Gertrude and Edgar Evans Cayce) has a quality in expressions alone that I feel fits the title, "Subject Patience." No comma there so read it again. Gertrude's hat reminds me of early Mexican caballero hats, and I really like the boy's casual headgear, don't you?

An immediate eyecatcher, the original fully colored same-size photograph as is this example of another co-operative Cayce effort, wherein Gertrude finished it in oil colors. Other than the lovely girl's name, there were no details around which we might at least imagine an interesting story. Those were real flowers . . . plastics were still in the future.

Edgar's greatest morale supporter and inspiration, his mother, obviously was thoroughly enjoying this picture-taking session with her grandson, Hugh Lynn. In evaluating all aspects of this and the portrait of Carrie Elizabeth Cayce you saw a few pages earlier, I tend to believe both were done during one sitting. There is little doubt that the year was early 1911, when Edgar was lured back to Hopkinsville by Dr. Ketchum, which would make this youngster four years of age. Removal of fungus, or mold, from the original print was too gigantic an undertaking, so I left it alone.

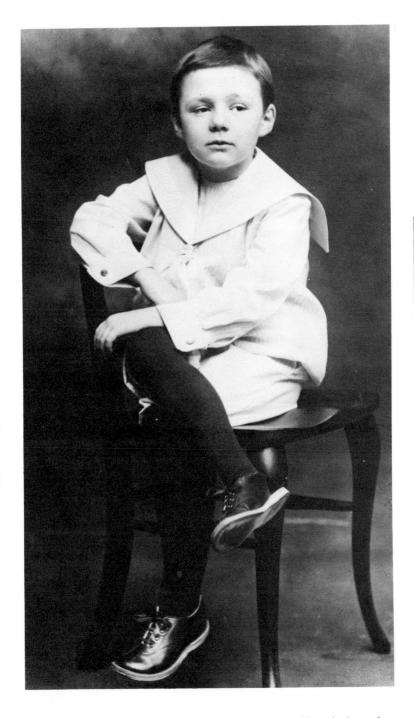

You older entities will more readily relate to my title for this priceless photographic pose by our hero (show business reference, "Ham"): "Seated Ham with Crossed Legs." It is doubtful that Edgar Cayce was seeking or encouraging the expression he captured here on his son's face. Perhaps it was stimulated through his suggesting a change of pose that young Hugh Lynn felt was unnecessary to a photographic model of his background and vast experience. This setting was a commercial effort, probably an advertising piece for this clothing that seems to have been inspired by Little Lord Fauntleroy, as popular an inspirational public image figure then as Superman, Walt Disney characters, Peanuts, etc., are today.

Just because I used this photograph to illustrate that newspaper article in the early Alabama period didn't mean I would not use it again here. No, I believe that was more of a Buffalo Bill, or possibly Wild Bill Hickok outfit, not a Boy Scout uniform— although Hugh Lynn did become active in the Boy Scout movement and a Scoutmaster in later years at Virginia Beach.

This woman of beauty, poise, character, strength, and fine intellect, chose an equally unique man with whom she would spend her whole life, and not until in her early forties did she learn (through those early Cayce life readings, for most of which she was the conductor) that she had made this choice prior to entering this lifetime. Here is Gertrude Cayce at the time Edgar opened his studio in Selma, and photographed by him, naturally.

The reader will undoubtedly speculate that this cute portrait of "Ecken" was made about, or possibly at the same sitting time as the previous one with his mother. Again, our photographer was practicing his new-found technique of eliminating all unwanted background, about which we'll write more later. Even under magnification, I was unable to determine what precious personal possession our little subject clutches tightly in his hands.

Another portrait of the "light of his life," Edgar Cayce's beloved mother . . . or so she was all-inspirational until Gertrude S. Evans became an influence with which to be reckoned. This portrait, you may have noticed earlier, hung next to that of her husband on the wall of Edgar's office, directly above his desk.

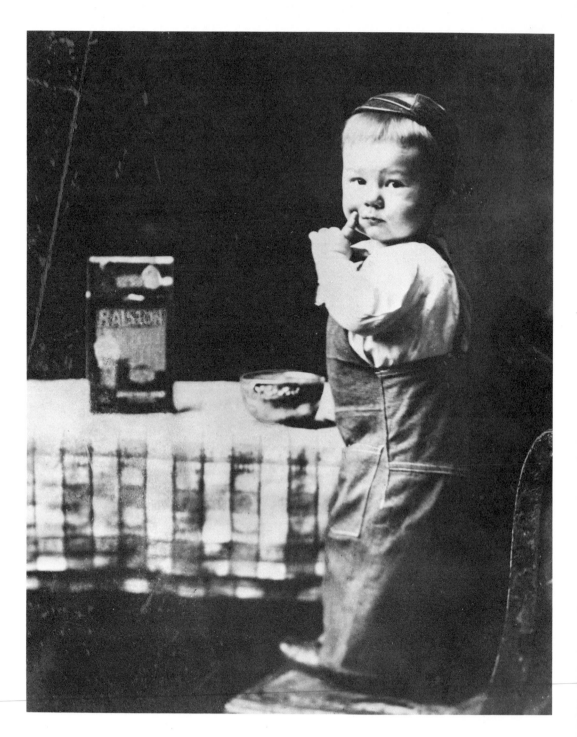

Whether or not it was classified as such in those days, Edgar Cayce produced considerable commercial photographic work. Hugh Lynn still strikes this same thoughtful pose today, often while lecturing, but never while standing on a kitchen chair (Sally Cayce frowns on such character display). Again, this was not the purchase pose, or if it was it deteriorated worse than I thought. Some object had adhered to a portion of the picture and tore away much of the emulsion in tiny particles, which had to be restored, including the brand name, Ralston, on the breakfast cereal box. An enchanting picture, at any rate.

Another portrait from the Cayce office wall (shown earlier) is this delightful semi-profile of Edgar's fiancée, whom he photographed for the forthcoming Pembroke historical publication (in one place it was called a magazine and in another "book" was its reference), in which Gertrude's portrait was slated to appear with three others he had photographed under the heading, "Some of Pembroke's Fair Ladies."

A mother and baby generally create interest almost any time or place, whether live or photographed. Edgar Cayce's rapport with children of all ages made for happy results, accounting for this very young one's concentration on the cameraman's position. This fine photographic example was one of perhaps eighteen glass-base negatives uncovered by William T. Turner, Hopkinsville historian, part of the same grouping used earlier in the book showing Hopkinsville businesses, stores, and parlor interiors. This portrait does have a flaw! A double image, caused by one or two possible oversights, doesn't actually ruin the finished product for its intended purpose here, although it may have been unacceptable to the subject-customer.

Occasionally, the subject was printed through a handmade mask, most often in the shape of an oval, and it served as a finished product (you saw a number of these examples early in the book). However, in this instance, because of their ceremonial attire, it is possible that the boys' parents may have asked for a full-length image, as you now see it.

This unusual portrait fascinates me . . . you, too? The lovely subject, by coincidence, is Sarah Cayce Hesson, Edgar's "baby" sister, who may not condone that pronoun. This picture was contributed by Sarah herself, along with many other photographs you have already seen.

I get the feeling from this portrait of Elizabeth E. Evans (Gertrude's mother) that she was the kind of person who wanted no modernistic approach, or the unusual, in photographic finishing, and possibly asked that hers be a simple and plain in-folder portrait, which is just what she got with this. I'm not criticizing the Cayce workmanship because the lighting, for example, is excellent, and I had little or no restoration to make, but I find it a little out of character for him.

225

"Kentuckians"

Photo Copy. Edgar Cayce 1906.

The colorful original of this obviously commercial endeavor is framed and hangs in Sally and Hugh Lynn Cayce's home. According to Gladys Davis' notation (across left-hand end of opposite postcard), Carrie Salter was responsible for the original painting and tinted the photocopy print prior to the postcard production.

(Above left) Gertrude's hurried note to the new father about this five-month-old son's condition, written on one of the "Kentuckians" postcards. (Above right) Gladys Davis' notation was probably added in the late '40s and is not part of the original postcard message. Restoration efforts to bring out the faded handwriting caused grayness around it.

(Right) This charming portrait was from another series of pictures produced primarily for beauty contest eliminations, a procedure that came about in many cities all over the United States. The lovely young woman you see here passed the many elimination tests and went on to become "Miss Selma" in the eventual Miss America national pageant.

Parade time! A most auspicious occasion for an enterprising young photographer, this day or days (in some areas this near-carnival atmosphere encompasses many days, excluding preparatory activity) being historical and possibly an only happenstance for our hero. However, you view here possibly one-tenth of the Cayce Art Company's total efforts for the community activity.

"Disciples," a title your compiler came up with when this fine photograph was exhibited (along with eight others in this group you've already viewed) for three months in the A.R.E. Headquarters lobby, summer 1971. In its time, this imaginative photograph was an award winner. The master artisan certainly expressed a message in this, his finest accomplishment, an opinion shared by his family and a select few who have previously seen it. Naturally, the original "Disciples" hangs reverently in the home of Sally and Hugh Lynn Cayce today.

(Opposite page) As with the first picture of Edgar's mother, this fine portrait of the exquisite bride, Gertrude Evans Cayce (photographed by the bridegroom himself . . . note monogram in lower left-hand corner), was acquired from Hugh Lynn's office. Prominently exhibited therein, it is Hugh Lynn's most precious memento, and as mentioned early in the book, he didn't want it included here when I first began compiling. His beautiful secretary, Norrene Leary, convinced him that it would be most appropriate to close the book with Gertrude's image, just as we opened it with Edgar's self-portrait. However, the idea, though not this particular photographic choice, was suggested by Edgar Evans Cayce, following his official scrutinization of this compilation as the A.R.E. Manuscript Committee representative. After all, let's not forget that this was his beloved mother, too.